GROWING UP
CHRISTIAN

GROWING UP
CHRISTIAN

Have You Taken Ownership of Your Relationship with God?

KARL GRAUSTEIN WITH MARK JACOBSEN

P U B L I S H I N G
P.O. BOX 817 • PHILLIPSBURG • NEW JERSEY 08865-0817

Page design and typesetting by Lakeside Design Plus

Printed in the United States of America

Library of Congress Cataloging-in-Publication Data

Graustein, Karl, 1971–
    Growing up Christian : have you taken ownership of your relationship with God? / Karl Graustein with Mark Jacobsen.
        p. cm.
    Includes bibliographical references (p.).
    ISBN-13: 978-087552-611-9 (paper)
    ISBN-10: 0-87552-611-X (paper)
    1. Christian teenagers—Religious life. I. Jacobsen, Mark, 1980– II. Title.

BV4531.3.G73 2005
248.8'3—dc22
                                                        2005047679

To my wonderful wife Jen, God's precious gift to me.

CONTENTS

Part 3 Living Biblically

ACKNOWLEDGMENTS

Thanks . . .

To Mark Jacobsen for writing the opening stories to each chapter. Thanks as well for editing the entire book and keeping the message clear and precise. God has given you a wonderful gift of writing. It has been a privilege and a joy to work with you.

To the staff at P&R for taking a chance on this first-time author. I greatly respect your commitment to publishing quality books for the body of Christ. Thanks in particular to Melissa Craig, Tara Davis, and Allan Fisher.

To Joshua Harris for inspiring and encouraging me in this project. It was the summer of 1999 when we first sat down and you encouraged me to put my thoughts into a book. Over the years you have met with me and given me essential advice and guidance. Thanks as well for endorsing the book.

To Jeff Myers, Marvin Olasky, Ken Smitherman, and Tedd Tripp for taking the time in your very busy schedules to read and then endorse this book.

To the leaders of Sovereign Grace Ministries for allowing me to include the lyrics to twelve Sovereign Grace worship songs. Thanks as well for allowing readers to download a free MP3 version of one song. I highly respect your mission and purpose, and I pray that the gospel is spread worldwide through your ministry.

To the leadership of Covenant Life Church for faithfully teaching and living according to the truths of Scripture. Thank you for modeling for me passionate worship and faithful pursuit of Christ.

To the students, faculty, and staff of Covenant Life School for supporting me throughout the writing process. Students, I highly respect you and enjoy watching you grow in your knowledge of God and love for the Savior. Faculty and staff, it is an honor to serve with you.

To Janeen Buck for editing early versions of this book. Your questions and advice gave invaluable direction to my writing.

To Tammy Stoy for carefully editing many chapters of the book. Your counsel kept me focused on the needs of young people growing up in the church.

To Carolyn McCulley for answering my many questions with wisdom and grace. Thanks for passing on to me much of what you have learned in your career and your writing experience.

To the many adults who reviewed proposals, chapters, or the entire book: Joshua Harris, Carolyn McCulley, Mark Lauterbach, Joe Lee, Tami Holmes, and Dave Brewer. Thank you for the large amount of time you devoted to review the book. Your comments and corrections made this book clearer, more biblically sound, and more effective.

To the teenagers who reviewed the book: Kate Greasely, Rachel Quinones, Crystal Quinones, Jeffrey Martin, and Paul-William deSilva. As part of my target audience, your feedback was encouraging and quite helpful.

To my "prayer team," Judy Furnish, Chung-Hae Casler, and Sue Robb, for praying for me. Your devotion to the Savior and your commitment to prayer inspire me.

To my parents, Alan and Joan Graustein, for sharing the gospel with me, teaching me the truths of Scripture, and inspiring me to run hard after Christ. Thanks as well for your countless prayers, your strong support for this project, and for reading and reviewing chapters of the book. I highly respect and love you.

To my dear wife Jen, my editor-in-chief, my number one supporter. I am so grateful to God for you. Thank you for encouraging and supporting me in countless ways over the years as this idea grew in my heart, as it became a reality, and as I devoted much time to writing.

Thank you for the many times you watched the kids so I could write. Thank you for being the first to read and review each chapter. Thanks for keeping me on target and for helping me clearly communicate my points. I could not have completed this project without you. I love you so much!

To my heavenly Father for laying this message on my heart. Thanks for giving me the privilege of growing up in a Christian home and working with young people who are doing the same. Thank you for allowing me to hear and respond to the gospel as a child. Thank you for fanning the flame of my faith my entire life. Thank you for placing the message of this book on my heart. Please use it as a way to get at the hearts and minds of church kids throughout the world.

PART 1 RECOGNIZING BLESSINGS AND DANGERS

But as for you, continue in what you have learned and have become convinced of, because you know those from whom you learned it, and how from infancy you have known the holy Scriptures, which are able to make you wise for salvation through faith in Christ Jesus.

—2 TIMOTHY 3:14–15

Lord, help me to

- appreciate the many blessings of growing up in a Christian home.

- have a faith and a walk of my own.

- recognize and avoid the unique challenges that church kids face.

- learn and grow as I read this book.

1 CHURCH KIDS

THE DYNAMICS OF GROWING UP CHRISTIAN

Saturday—1:00 A.M.

This is wrong.

Kara's conscience seemed to roar through the dark, silent house. She cringed and froze midstep, heart thundering so loudly she felt certain the sound would awaken her parents. When she'd made her plans this morning, sneaking out hadn't seemed like a big deal, but now the fear and guilt were so overwhelming, she thought she might throw up.

She spotted movement in the living room, and jumped a foot off the ground. For one horrified moment she was convinced that her father was sitting in his easy chair; then she realized that it was just a shadow shifting across the floor, as tree branches swayed outside the window. She gulped an uneasy breath. Kara had no idea what her punishment would be if her parents caught her, but she knew they would be disappointed in her. That was an awful thought. She suddenly wanted more than anything to go upstairs and crawl back into bed, but then she thought of Nick sitting in his Mustang waiting for her. She couldn't just ditch him tonight. She'd promised.

When Kara had met Nick at a youth-group retreat last June, she'd never imagined things taking this turn. Both were sincere Christians who had strong convictions about their faith and their integrity. They even led worship together at Sunday evening youth group, but lately Kara's grades had been slipping, and her parents and friends were getting concerned about the amount of time that she and Nick were spending together. Two weeks ago, her parents had tightened her curfew and placed some limits on how much time she could spend with Nick. Kara knew they were trying to protect her, but she loved Nick, and the new rules seemed unreasonable. Last week she'd broken them twice. Worse, she'd lied to her parents about where she'd been. Tonight, sneaking out in the middle of the night, things were taking an even worse turn. Kara felt awful. She knew the guilt would be especially acute tomorrow evening, when she and Nick stood up to lead worship at youth group.

It felt so hard being a teenager and a Christian. She wanted to honor God and her parents, but living a Christian life in the twenty-first century seemed like an uphill battle. Her parents didn't seem to understand, just slapped down rules. Why couldn't they just let her lead her own life? Sure, she might make some mistakes, but things would work themselves out. Besides, it wasn't like Nick was a bad guy. He was a Christian, so why did her parents have to be so restrictive?

It was their fault that she had to sneak out like this, Kara told herself. They weren't leaving her any other choice. She furrowed her brow with resolve and tiptoed to the door.

Salvation

"There's more to life than baseball," Brian said through his mouthful of Egg McMuffin. He and Matt were huddled over their breakfast in a corner of the restaurant, which was bustling with other friends and families grabbing their pre-church breakfast and coffee.

"Not my life," Matt retorted. They both laughed. Matt's name was practically synonymous with baseball. He'd been playing since age eight, and was presently the starting shortstop on his college team. When he wasn't playing, he was training. You couldn't talk to him without being barraged by the latest news from the sports page. Matt lived for the game.

This Sunday, however, Matt's laughter only thinly veiled his unease. He'd been meeting with Brian every Sunday morning for two months now, and their conversations had probed progressively deeper. Their small talk about baseball, college, and friends had steadily yielded to Brian's favorite subject: his faith in God. Matt had always thought of himself as a Christian, so he dismissed much of this talk as being familiar turf. After all, his parents were Christians and he regularly attended church. He had a Bible and knew most of the stories. What more did Brian really have to say?

But something was different today. Matt felt a sense of awe as Brian described the significance and meaning he attached to his faith. It was no casual belief. Brian's faith defined his life. And Brian was *cool*. Matt had grown up around plenty of adult Christians, but he'd never met a Christian like Brian, someone his own age who was joyful and intelligent and had such passion and certainty about his life. Matt had come to deeply respect his friend. He wanted what Brian had. Every word Brian spoke this morning seemed to pierce his heart.

Brian was right. Matt knew he had been defining his life by the wrong things. Now, as he spoke with Brian, he sensed the light of a new dawn breaking in his heart. Brian had shown him that genuine, deep, and significant faith was within his reach. The excitement rose in his soul. He had to tell Brian what he was feeling.

Matt set aside the remains of his forgotten sandwich, leaned eagerly across the table, and started to share.

Popularity

Every girl in Jackson Community College seemed to be enamored of Eric. Every day when Tim walked into his freshman literature class, he saw a whole pack of them surrounding Eric's desk, giggling and smiling and throwing him shy looks. It was unbelievable. Less than two weeks into the school year, and Eric already had the standing of a Greek god. He was popular with the guys, too. Tim never saw him without a gaggle of worshipful, tagalong friends. Tim couldn't blame

17

them. Eric had it all: six-foot-three, linebacker on the football team, a charming sense of humor, and a heavily muscled body.

Tim took a seat in the back corner of the classroom and watched as Eric recounted one of his drunken escapades from Friday's party. Guys and girls alike erupted in riotous laughter. Tim sighed with envy.

Tim had always been in the popular crowd at his Christian high school, where he'd played sports, served in the student government, and led Bible studies. He'd had high expectations of celebrating his newfound freedom and new friends in college, but so far, he just felt lost in the crowd. Hardly anybody knew who he was. Tim was quickly discovering that his faith didn't earn him much popularity here because Christians were few and far between, and the popular circles mostly revolved around the party scene.

The fact was, he just wasn't enjoying his college life so far. Serious Christianity and secular college didn't seem to mix well. Maybe he should loosen up a little. He was young and still learning about himself, so why couldn't he experiment? That's what college was about, right? There would be time to get serious later. Why not enjoy himself now?

Eric cracked a crude joke, and the gathering around his desk laughed once more. Tim found himself laughing, too. Eric *was* funny. Tim looked around, took a deep breath, then rose to join the circle. Maybe he could learn a few things from Eric.

Can you relate to Kara, Matt, or Tim? Kara had a strong, sincere faith, but found herself increasingly ensnared in sin. Matt had always considered himself a Christian, but at the age of 19 he realized that he wasn't. Tim claimed to be a Christian, but his craving for popularity led to serious compromises when he reached college. Each had grown up in a Christian home, yet faced particular challenges and temptations. They were church kids wrestling with the desires of their hearts, trying to find their true identities.

What's a Church Kid?

Once, I spoke at a high school leadership conference where a few of the teenagers didn't like the term "church kids." To them it had the same connotations as "pastor's kids," a term often synonymous with troublemakers. Maybe you feel the same way, but when you really understand what a church kid is, I think you will see that it's an overwhelmingly positive term.

Church kids are individuals who have grown up in the church. They come from Christian homes, have Christian parents, and have attended church their entire lives. They live in a Christian culture surrounded by Christians at home, church, and often school. It is a wonderful privilege to be a church kid.

I'm a church kid myself, and I am incredibly grateful to God for the many blessings we church kids experience while growing up in Christian homes. We have been raised and trained by godly parents; we have been repeatedly told the message of the gospel; we have been taught the Word of God from a young age; we have regularly attended church where we have worshiped God and have been taught about his character; we have lots of Christian friends; and we have been protected from many of the negative influences of the world.

In July of 1971, God greatly blessed me by allowing me to be born into a strong Christian family in a small town in New Hampshire. My parents had not grown up in Christian homes, but God had saved them about six years before I was born. They faithfully raised me according to biblical principles. Our family regularly attended church, prayed together, and had times of family Bible study. My parents sent me to youth-group meetings, a Christian school, and a Christian college. I grew up a fairly typical church kid.

Just before I turned four, in July of 1975, God drew me to himself through the gentle teaching and leading of my parents. At that time I repented of my sins and professed Jesus as my personal Savior. I had a four-year-old's understanding of the gospel and, in retrospect, I think a genuine conversion. (Isn't it amazing that the gospel message is simple enough for a four year old to grasp!) I do not remember the time prior to my salvation. I practically grew up a Christian.

19

As I grew older, my faith steadily grew, too. God used specific trials in elementary and high school to refine my faith and teach me how to trust him. After high school, I left rural New Hampshire and headed to the suburbs of Chicago to attend Wheaton College, where God helped me begin to live out my faith and form a walk of my own. He also confirmed a call on my life to work in Christian education, and since graduating in 1993, I have worked full-time as a teacher and principal in a Christian school.

I am a church kid. I grew up surrounded by church kids, went to college with church kids, and have worked closely with church kids for the past twelve years. I have experienced and observed both the blessings and the dangers of growing up in a Christian environment, and I have a strong desire that church kids learn to praise God for the privileges they experience and to carefully navigate the dangers they face.

Blessings

Growing up in a Christian home is a wonderful privilege. We have been given so much: godly parents, training in the Word of God, friends from Christian homes, support from a Christian church community, and most importantly an opportunity to know God at a young age. Throughout our lives, we are repeatedly taught about the love of God, his plan of salvation, ways to recognize and resist sin, and living for the glory of God.

Not only are we given much, we are also protected from much. Our God-fearing and loving parents wisely limit our entertainment options—television, music, movies, books, and magazines. They carefully monitor our friendships and our exposure to the message of the world. We learn about the lies of secular values and other religions. We are trained to evaluate all of life according to the standards of Scripture.

Daily, I benefit from years of being taught the truths of Scripture and from countless hours of reading the Word. My parents have provided for me a clear example of living all of life for the glory of God, maintaining a strong marriage, and raising children. Because of faithful training by my parents, teachers, and church leaders, I have not had to break many bad habits and regret years of godless living.

I have a friend who became a Christian at the age of 41. He is determined to live every moment of his life for God because he feels like he wasted his first 41 years. My friend wishes he had had the opportunities of the young people in his church. He sees how they know more about God than he does at only a third of his age, and he gets excited about the difference they will make for Christ as they move into adulthood.

When I think that I have lived thirty years as a Christian and (Lord willing) may live another fifty years, I'm amazed at God's love and kindness toward me. It truly is a great blessing to be a church kid.

Dangers

Church kids do face some unique challenges like the ones Kara, Matt, and Tim encountered. Though surrounded by the things of God, we, like Kara, can still be drawn to sin and live double lives; like Matt, we can easily assume that we are saved even if we are not; or, like Tim,

---

THINK ABOUT IT

J. C. Ryle reminds us of the privilege of having religious parents and warns us about the dangers we face:

I ask the children of religious parents to mark well what I am saying. It is the highest privilege to be the child of a godly father and mother, and to be brought up in the midst of many prayers. It is a blessed thing indeed to be taught the gospel from our earliest infancy, and to hear of sin, and Jesus, and the Holy Spirit, and holiness, and heaven, from the first moment we can remember anything. But, oh, take heed that you do not remain barren and unfruitful in the sunshine of all these privileges: beware lest your heart remains hard, impenitent, and worldly, notwithstanding the many advantages you enjoy. You cannot enter the kingdom of God on the credit of your parents' religion. You must eat the bread of life for yourself, and have the witness of the Spirit in your own heart. You must have repentance of your own, faith of your own, and sanctification of your own.[1]—J. C. Ryle

---

we may be driven by a desire to be popular more than a desire to live according to biblical values. While it is a great blessing to grow up in a Christian environment, if we are not careful we can make some dangerous assumptions about ourselves, which have serious consequences.

I know firsthand what it is like to simply copy our parents' beliefs and convictions. I know how difficult it can be to live according to the standards of the Bible and our parents. I know what it is like to obey simply to avoid punishment instead of truly wanting to please God or my parents. I have had friends who appeared to be Christians in high school, but later walked away from their faith. I've known individuals who have partied on Saturday night and put on their Sunday best for church the next morning. I have observed students act one way when an adult is present and completely differently when they think no one is watching. I have watched students be attracted to the values and practices of the world around them and believe the lies the world promotes. I have had students lie to me in an attempt to avoid discipline.

Take His Word for It

Timothy

Scripture is full of stories of individuals with religious parents—Isaac, Jacob, Solomon, and Eli's sons—who serve as both good and bad examples for us. Some had genuine faith and accomplished much for God, while others had no relationship with God and were wicked. We can learn a lot from each of these individuals.

A negative example that should sober us is the story of Samuel's sons, Joel and Abijah. Samuel lived an amazing life, serving as God's representative to the people of Israel. He was recognized as a godly man who spoke directly to God and heard directly from God. There is no doubt he had a genuine faith. But when we look at his sons, it is clear that their faith was different. They didn't walk in the ways Samuel walked. Instead, "They turned aside after dishonest gain and accepted bribes and perverted justice" (1 Sam. 8:3).

On the other hand, the story of Timothy should inspire us. Although his father was a Greek, his mother and grandmother were Jewish Christians who taught him Scripture from a young age (2 Tim. 3:15). Paul

22

said of Timothy's faith, "I have been reminded of your sincere faith, which first lived in your grandmother Lois and in your mother Eunice and, I am persuaded, now lives in you also" (2 Tim. 1:5). Timothy had a personal faith that was genuine and commendable, and Paul wanted to take him along on his second missionary journey (Acts 16:3).

We can also learn a lot from Paul's two letters to Timothy. Although Timothy had traveled extensively with Paul, Paul eventually left him in Ephesus to lead and care for the Ephesian church. Both letters were written toward the end of Paul's life. Second Timothy may even be Paul's last letter, written from jail just before he was martyred.

Paul knew of Timothy's training. Paul saw the fruit of Timothy's mother and grandmother, who had read and explained holy Scripture to Timothy. Paul saw the strong biblical foundation Timothy had, and he remembered Timothy's amazement as Paul preached about Jesus Christ and the message of the gospel. So Paul urged Timothy to continue in his faith, remembering who had taught him the truths of God. Paul wanted Timothy to look back at his training, remember the people God had used, and recall the truths taught to him so that Timothy could live passionately for God.

Our situation is similar to Timothy's. We have a religious heritage, having been trained in the truths of Scripture from infancy. Our parents read to us—countless times—the stories of the Bible. They have taught us about God, his plan of salvation, and how to live godly lives. We need to look back at our training and the people God used to teach us, appreciating the great blessing we have in growing up in a Christian home. We, too, need to continue in the faith, seek to grow in our love for our Savior, and become church kids on fire for God.

> **THINK ABOUT IT**
> Paul's words were written for Timothy, but also speak to us today:
>
> But as for you, continue in what you have learned and have become convinced of, because you know those from whom you learned it, and how from infancy you have known the holy Scriptures, which are able to make you wise for salvation through faith in Christ Jesus. (2 Tim. 3:14–15)

We need the same attitude as Paul: "I press on to take hold of that for which Christ Jesus took hold of me. . . . Forgetting what is behind and straining toward what is ahead, I press on toward the goal to win the prize for which God has called me heavenward in Christ Jesus" (Phil. 3:12–14).

Straining toward what is ahead and pressing on toward the goal, we must have our own faith, our own passion, and our own walk with God. Empowered by the Holy Spirit, we need to live every aspect of our lives for the glory of God.

A Look in the Mirror

You're a Church Kid If . . .

So would you say that you are a church kid? If yes, please understand the favor God has shown in allowing you to grow up in a Christian environment, and know that you do face some unique challenges. You have benefited greatly from godly parents who deeply love you

---

THINK ABOUT IT

How do you know if you are a church kid? You're a church kid if many of these statements apply to you:

Check each statement that applies to you.

Your parents are Christians.

Your parents became Christians before you were born.

You have considered yourself a Christian for most of your life.

You have attended church most of your life.

You regularly attend youth-group meetings or other church ministry meetings.

You often read the Bible.

You know most of the stories of the Bible.

You often pray.

Your family has family Bible studies.

Most of your friends are Christians.

You attend a Christian school or you are homeschooled.

---

and desire that you love and obey God. Yet your life and faith are different from those of your parents and others who became Christians as adults. This book is designed to help you become aware of these differences. It will help you understand your tendencies so that you can accurately know your heart and live in a way that truly pleases God.

If you are a teenager and you are not a church kid, please know that there is still much for you in this book. Even if you cannot relate to the characteristics listed above, but you are currently attending church and youth group, the truths outlined in this book will benefit you. Even if you are not a typical church kid, but you are a young person growing up in the church, the themes of this book apply directly to you.

What about You?

Church kids may grow up in similar environments (Christian homes and church every week), but our hearts, thoughts, and lives can vary significantly. Some church kids are genuinely saved at a young age while others may not truly believe until they are adults. Many are saved and growing in their love for God, others may be saved but not growing much at all, and some are not even saved. Some take their sin seriously while others do not even see their sin. Some trust God from their hearts while others constantly worry.

What about you? How would you describe yourself?

- Are you on fire for God?
- Are you for the first time realizing that you may not be a Christian?
- Are you beginning to take your personal relationship with God more seriously?
- Does your life resemble the values of the world more than the Word?
- Do you love holiness and hate sin? Do you strive to fight the sin of your heart and not simply address your sinful behaviors?
- Do you like attending church?
- Do you appreciate and obey your parents?
- Do you enjoy reading and studying the Bible?

- Are you prepared for the new freedoms in your life now that you're getting older?
- Do you have strong personal convictions?
- Are you getting ready to head off to college and move away from your family for the first time in your life?
- Are you experiencing significant anxiety as you think of the future?

Church kids come in all types of shapes and sizes. Although we all grow up in Christian homes, our hearts can be in very different places. Although we have known about God most of our lives, our love for him can vary greatly. Although we know the Bible, our pursuit of thinking and living biblically can vary significantly.

Taking Your Faith to the Next Level

This book is for individuals who have grown up in Christian homes and who want to take their faith to the next level. It is for young adults who realize their responsibility to take hold of their personal relationship with God. It is a book that describes the unique perspective and tendencies of church kids. It is filled with warnings as well as practical suggestions for growth in godliness. It contains biblical truths that will guide individuals in thinking and living in a way that pleases God.

Here are some of the themes we will explore in the three sections of this book:

Part 1 explains some of the dangers church kids face. We'll learn of the danger of assuming we are saved when we are not. We'll discover that an improper view of our sin leads to a dangerous lack of appreciation for the saving and forgiving grace of God. We'll understand the dangerous effects of loving and pursuing the world. We'll learn about each of these dangers and concentrate on biblical ways to avoid each of them.

Part 2 goes on the offensive. We'll learn the importance of thinking biblically. We'll start by learning how biblical greatness requires a humble heart. We'll explore the necessity of developing personal convictions based on the Word of God. We'll look at the importance of being grateful for God, the Bible, our parents, and our church. We'll examine the importance of trusting in God. We'll discover the freedom and strength that comes from pursuing sound, biblical doctrine. We'll realize that thinking biblically is the first step toward living biblically.

Part 3 urges us to put into practice what we know and demonstrate our love for God through obedience. We'll examine the seriousness of our sin and specific methods to battle our sin at the heart level. We'll discover the need to passionately practice the spiritual disciplines. We'll understand the many opportunities we have to carefully steward our God-given talents. Ultimately, we'll learn what it means to live biblically.

A Call to Action

As a church kid, you have been entrusted with many blessings and privileges. If you recognize the blessings and carefully navigate the dangers, you will be prepared to make a great difference for Christ and his kingdom. If you learn to think and live biblically, you will be a passionate church kid on fire for God.

Commit today to:

√ Be grateful to God for the many blessings of growing up in a Christian home
√ Recognize and avoid the unique challenges that you face
√ Take personal ownership of your faith and your relationship with God
√ Think and live in a way that pleases God

Questions for Reflection and Discussion

1. What is a church kid?
2. Are you a church kid? Which qualities of a church kid apply to your life? In what ways is your experience different?

3. What are some of the blessings of growing up in a Christian home?

4. What are some challenges that church kids face?

5. What did Paul mean when he told Timothy to "continue in what you have learned and have become convinced of, because you know those from whom you learned it"?

6. The subtitle of this book asks, "Have you taken ownership of your relationship with God?" What does this mean? What is your answer?

7. Part 2 of this book is titled "Thinking Biblically" and part 3 is titled "Living Biblically." What is the connection between thinking biblically and living biblically?

8. What do you hope to gain from reading this book?

Sing a New Song

"Haven't You Been Good"[2]

Thank You for the cross
Thank You Lord for drawing me
Out of millions lost
Thank You Lord for saving me
Haven't You been good
Haven't You been so good

Chorus
Glory to Your name
Glory to Your holy name
Thankfulness and praise
For grace and mercy never changing
Haven't You been good
Haven't You been so good to me

Favor on my life
Always watching over me
My darkness turned to light
And heaven's are enfolding me
Haven't you been good
Haven't You been so good

For more information on this song, go to www.growingupchristian.com.

Examine yourselves to see whether you are in the faith; test yourselves. Do you not realize that Christ Jesus is in you—unless, of course, you fail the test?

—2 CORINTHIANS 13:5

Lord,

- help me to clearly see the current state of my heart.

- give me saving faith—if I don't already have it.

- grant me true assurance of salvation.

- help me to grow in my appreciation for the gospel message.

2 IN OR OUT?

THE DANGER OF FALSE ASSURANCE

Family Man

Robert was the kind of next-door neighbor every suburban family wants. Friends and neighbors described him as a patriot, quiet professional, and family man. His reputation in the community was exemplary. He was intelligent and well educated, with a master's degree in accounting and information systems and experience as an accountant in Chicago. He was also a man of character and conviction; for three years he'd served on the Chicago police force, weeding out crooked cops. After that, he'd gone on to work in government law enforcement, landing a job at the state department in Washington, D.C. People slept better at night with a guy like that on the block.

Robert's deep religious convictions left an impression on his coworkers and neighbors. He was a devoted member of the Catholic Church, as well as a conservative organization within the church called Opus Dei. At times he boldly extended his convictions into the workplace, challenging coworkers regarding what he believed were sinful behaviors.[1] If you walked past his comfortable brick home on any given Sunday, you would see him loading his wife and six kids into their modest van. "All eight of them [go] to mass without fail,"[2] one neighbor commented on the devout family. Another said, "The kids are great kids—well educated, polite, nice kids. It's just a great family."[3]

Then the bombshell dropped.

On February 18, 2001, neighbors awoke to see crime-scene tape surrounding Robert's home. Curiosity gave way to shock and horror as the story unfolded. Instead of celebrating his retirement in five weeks, this quiet, reserved father of six would be facing trial for treason. Robert Hanssen was a spy for Russia.

And he wasn't just any spy. "We are talking about the most prolific and damaging spy in U.S. history. Secrets [were] sold, not only from the FBI where he worked, but also from the CIA, the White House, the Pentagon and the National Security Agency,"[4] said David Vise, the *Washington Post* reporter covering the story at the time.

Over a period of almost twenty years, Hanssen had given the Soviets (later the Russians) more than six thousand pages of classified documents, escalating the possibility of nuclear war. Among these documents were U.S. plans in the event of a Soviet attack, and the names of individuals working as spies for the United States (at least two of whom were subsequently executed). He also handed off national-security software that al Qaeda terrorists may have purchased from a Russian individual while planning the September 11, 2001 attacks. The consequences of Hanssen's betrayal were catastrophic and far-reaching.

For over twenty years, one of the most serious spies in U.S. history had masked his treachery behind the guise of a quiet, principled family man. He knew how to put on a good show to fool friends and neighbors, but his most private thoughts and actions revealed a very different man.

We can do a similar thing as church kids. Many of us have been raised in a Christian tradition. We know the right answers in Sunday school, the right way to speak and act around Christians, the right attitudes to convey. We have the Christian "image" down to a fine art. Yet not all of us really believe the things we profess, and often our inmost thoughts reveal very different convictions.

What are your secret prayers and thoughts? Would it surprise anyone in your life if they knew your true desires and opinions? Are you really who everyone thinks you are?

It is possible to fool those closest to us. It is even possible to be fooled ourselves, which brings us to the first danger church kids encounter.

Danger #1

The most significant danger church kids face is false assurance of salvation—assuming that we are saved even when we are not.

We grow up in a Christian culture with Christians all around us—family, church, and friends. Because we do the things Christians do and we are surrounded by Christians, we tend to assume we are Christians, too. But just as standing in a wheatfield doesn't make someone wheat, being raised in a Christian environment doesn't make someone a Christian.

What gives you confidence that you are a Christian? The list on the next page refers primarily to external actions. Each could in fact be a fruit of salvation—a good work or action of a believer. But each could also be nothing more than an unbeliever's conforming to his environment (to please parents, fit in with peers, etc.) while there is no saving faith in his heart.

Don't fall into the dangerous trap of false assurance. As you read this chapter, take some time to examine your relationship with God. Search your heart. Pray. Don't make the mistake of basing your salvation on what you do or your environment. Genuine salvation is a matter of the heart. It is based on faith alone—faith in God's character, his promises, and the work of his Son on the cross.

Take His Word for It

1. Salvation is a matter of the heart. Those of us who have grown up in Christian homes are well acquainted with verses such as John 3:16 ("For God so loved the world that he gave his one and only Son, that whoever believes in him shall not perish but have eternal life") and Romans 10:9 ("That if you confess with your mouth, 'Jesus is Lord,' and believe in your heart that God raised him from the dead, you will be saved"). We have read or heard these verses hundreds if not thousands of times. We understand that salvation is by faith, and we tend to think we have saving faith because we know key verses about the gospel. But knowing the facts of the gospel doesn't necessarily mean that we are true Christians.

THINK ABOUT IT

We tend to believe we are Christians because . . .

Our parents are Christians.
We believe God exists.
We faithfully attend church and youth meetings.
We pray.
We read and know much about the Bible.
We prayed the "sinner's prayer" or went forward during an altar call.
We were baptized.
We sing hymns and worship songs.
We listen to Christian music.
We are basically good, moral people, especially compared to the world.
We attend a Christian school or Christian college.

Just because we have ridden in a car doesn't mean that we are qualified to drive a car. In a sense, we have been passengers in the car of our parents' faith. We have observed how their personal relationship with God affects their lives. We have been beside them in times of prayer and family Bible studies, we have served with them, and we have traveled with them to church, prayer meetings, and outreach events. But just because we have seen their faith in action doesn't automatically mean that we have the same faith.

You see, salvation is a matter of *your* heart, not your parents' hearts. *You* must have faith. *You* must believe. Don't miss those important words in Romans 10:9: "believe in *your* heart."

Have you ever observed young children in a Sunday-school class? It seems like no matter the question they yell out "God!" or "Jesus!" for the answer—even when the correct answer is "Satan." From a young age, we learn to say the right things and give the right answers, which for the most part is a wonderful blessing. But the downside is that we can learn to say the right thing with the wrong heart motivation. We can even learn to live like a Christian without being a true Christian. Jesus rebuked the Pharisees for this type of living.

A true Christian is a Christian at heart. Genuine salvation requires personal faith. Although it can be easy for us to worship God with our lips or to say the right thing at the right time, that is not enough.

> **THINK ABOUT IT**
> We can learn from Jesus' warning:
>
> These people honor me with their lips, but their hearts are far from me. (Matt. 15:8)

Ultimately, salvation is about God's living in us, which then enables us to live the Christian life.

2. You can know if you are a true Christian. A few years ago, my brother's car suddenly began running poorly. It was not accelerating at its usual rate, and the engine knocked while it idled. His mechanic thought the car needed a tune-up, but the problems continued. About a week later, my brother happened to refuel at a different gas station, and within minutes his car began to run smoothly again. He quickly realized the problem had been a bad tank of gas.

Yet how did he know for sure? He didn't test the gas. If he had smelled it or looked at it, it would have seemed normal, but the car clearly had not been running normally. The only way to judge the quality of the gas was by the way the car functioned. Bad gasoline resulted in bad performance, and good gasoline resulted in good performance. The relationship between our heart and our walk with God is similar.

Like bad gasoline, an unregenerated heart will be apparent in our patterns of ungodly thoughts, words, and actions. And similar to the good gasoline, regenerated hearts will demonstrate a pattern of God-honoring thoughts, words, and actions.

Jesus compared people to fruit trees. A tree is determined to be good and healthy if it produces good fruit; conversely, a bad tree is known by its bad fruit. People are similar. In looking at an individual's life over a period of time, a careful observer will see fruit in keeping with salvation or actions that reflect a lack of salvation.

Discerning the difference can be particularly challenging for us who have grown up in Christian homes. If we take a superficial look at our lives, we will see actions and hear words that are normal for Christians. The key for us is to carefully examine the thoughts and motives behind our words and actions.

> **THINK ABOUT IT**
> We can tell whether God is living in us. Jesus said that we can know our true nature by looking at the fruit of our lives:
>
> No good tree bears bad fruit, nor does a bad tree bear good fruit. Each tree is recognized by its own fruit. . . . The good man brings good things out of the good stored up in his heart, and the evil man brings evil things out of the evil stored up in his heart. For out of the overflow of his heart his mouth speaks. (Luke 6:43–45)

It is one thing to attend church each week and quite another to want to go to church to encounter God in times of worship and teaching. It is one thing to simply sing hymns or worship songs and quite another to truly worship God with all our heart. It is one thing to pray before a meal or sit quietly when another person prays and quite another to earnestly seek God for direction, help, or comfort. It is one thing to simply read the Bible and quite another to seek to commune with God while studying Scripture. And it is one thing to do what our parents ask us to do and quite another to act in obedience out of a deep desire to please God and honor our parents. To correctly evaluate our hearts, we need to examine the thoughts and motives behind our words and actions.

What do your motives say about the state of your heart?

3. Your eternal destination is at stake. In Matthew 25:1–13, Jesus told a parable of ten virgins who went out to meet the bridegroom for a wedding ceremony. Five had wisely brought extra oil for their lamps, and five foolishly had not. While they waited, the foolish virgins ran out of oil and had to go out to buy more. When they returned, they learned that the bridegroom had arrived and the door to the wedding banquet had been shut. They cried out for the door to be opened, but the bridegroom said, "I tell you the truth, I don't know you." They were locked out.

Jesus told the story to urge us to be prepared for his return. We need to keep watch and be ready because when this life is over, there are only two outcomes: eternity with God and eternity without him.

Later, in Matthew 25:31–46, Jesus again illustrated our two eternal options when he told the story of the separation of the sheep and the goats. He used the sheep to represent the saved and the goats to represent the unsaved. To the sheep he will say, "Come, you who are blessed by my Father; take your inheritance, the kingdom prepared for you since the creation of the world" (v. 34). To the goats he will say, "Depart from me, you who are cursed, into the eternal fire prepared for the devil and his angels" (v. 41).

Jesus clearly distinguished between those who are considered righteous and will enter heaven and the unrighteous, who will be damned to hell. He made it clear that we have only one of two options: in or out. There is no middle ground.

What is your eternal destination? Are you sure?

A Look in the Mirror

Have you ever heard of the book *Christy*, by Catherine Marshall? It is the story of Christy Huddleston—a well-known church kid. At the age of 20, she had a wake-up call regarding her faith when she attended the funeral of a friend—a husband and father of six who had been murdered.

> By now I knew that my religion, inherited intact from my family, had been mostly [routine]. Little about it had penetrated to where I, Christy, really lived. Back home church services had all but anesthetized me; I had become wondrously adept at dialing my mind to "off" for every word that the minister said and all that went on in church services, and to "on" for whatever was more interesting to ponder. Already my brush with raw life in the mountains had blown away much fog. Either this Christianity was true—or it was not.[6]

Can you relate to these words? Has your Christianity penetrated to where you really live, or are you sitting numbly through church services, missing life-giving messages while you think about your sports game or social activities? Or as Charles Spurgeon asks, have tears and prayers and sermons been wasted on your barren heart?[7] Or are you so accustomed to hearing the gospel that your soul sleeps under it?[8]

> **THINK ABOUT IT**
> Examine yourselves to see whether you are in the faith; test yourselves. Do you not realize that Christ Jesus is in you—unless, of course, you fail the test? (2 Cor. 13:5–6)

The ultimate question is this: Do you see evidences of genuine salvation in your life? When you look closely at your heart and life, do you see consistent, godly fruit?

Let's take a moment to carefully examine our hearts by looking closely at our lives. It's time for a 2 Corinthians 13 self-test.

SELF-TEST

When you are by yourself . . .

Do you pray? What do you pray about?

Do you read the Bible? Do you enjoy reading your Bible? Do you experience God teaching you when you read your Bible?

Do you worship God? Why do you worship?

Do you think about God? What aspects of God do you think about?

Do you confess your sin to God?

YOUR MOTIVES

Why do you pray?

Why do you read your Bible?

Why do you go to church?

Why do you attend youth meetings?

What do you think about in times of corporate worship?

Why do you do good works?

Why do you acknowledge sin in your life?

Why do you obey your parents?

YOUR RELATIONSHIPS

Do you talk about God with your friends?

Do you tell non-Christians about your faith?

Do you have a good relationship with your parents?

Do you enjoy spending time with true Christians?

Do you desire to serve others?

What do you think? What does the fruit in your life say about your heart? What do the motives behind your words and actions say about your heart? When you ask yourself these questions and you consider your answers, can you say that you are truly saved?

Remember, it is God living and acting in our hearts that enables us to live in a way that pleases him. Our godly fruit is the result of salvation, not the source of salvation. Although a true Christian is far from perfect, patterns of godly thoughts, words, and actions are evidence of a regenerated heart. And conversely, a lack of good fruit is usually an indication of a heart that has not been transformed by God.

So far, we've examined how a lack of fruit indicates a lack of saving faith, but there's an exciting additional truth: consistent good fruit can bring us assurance of our salvation. I know church kids who feel guilty if they do not pray and read their Bibles every day or if they miss a youth meeting. They are the type of church kids who also tend to question their salvation even though they are true Christians. Scripture is clear that if this description fits you, you can have assurance of your salvation. If you are a genuine believer who trusts in Christ and can identify clear, godly fruit in your life, you should praise God and rest confidently in the great work he initiated in your heart.

> **THINK ABOUT IT**
>
> If we get it wrong about Jesus, it doesn't matter what else we get right.[9]—RANDY ALCORN

But what if you can't identify good fruit? What if you've always considered yourself a Christian, but now aren't so sure? In that case, please hear the heart of this chapter. Our greatest need is personal salvation. All other needs are secondary. Before *growing* in our relationship with God, we must *have* a relationship with him. It is meaningless to even address other needs before addressing our personal relationship with God. Without God and his enabling power, we cannot effectively change any part of our lives.

"Tell Me the Old, Old Story"

Now that we have examined our lives for signs of genuine salvation, we need to look in detail at the gospel. As we review the facts, may the unsaved be challenged to believe and those freshly assured of their salvation be encouraged.

If you are a church kid, you have heard the gospel many times in many ways. This won't be new to you. In fact, I know a pastor who affectionately refers to the gospel as "That Old, Old Story."[10] We can all benefit from a solid review of this old, old story. Consider again with me the gospel message.

A friend of mine sums up the condition of mankind with the short statement: "God is good; we are not; and that is bad." He succinctly describes the character of God, the nature of man, and the consequences to man. We need to understand all three of these elements to fully understand the message of the gospel. The more we learn about God—his character, attributes, and love for us—the more we will love him. The more we understand our sinful nature, the more we will see our need for our loving Savior.

What are the essential components of the gospel?

1. The character of God. The Bible describes God as holy (Ps. 99:3, 5, 9; Rev. 4:8), righteous (Ps. 11:7), just (2 Thess. 1:6), and perfect (Matt. 5:48). He hates sin and has nothing to do with it. In fact, he pours out his justified wrath on sin (Rom. 1:18; Eph. 5:6).

> **THINK ABOUT IT**
> Paul wonderfully captured the truths of the gospel in these two passages:
>
> For all have sinned and fall short of the glory of God, and are justified freely by his grace through the redemption that came by Christ Jesus. (Rom. 3:23–24)
>
> God made him who had no sin to be sin for us, so that in him we might become the righteousness of God. (2 Cor. 5:21)

2. The character and nature of man. At the same time, the Bible describes man as having a sinful nature (Ps. 51:5), hopelessly separated from God. We are unable to please God in and of ourselves (Rom. 8:8). We all have sinned and fallen short of the glory of God (Rom. 3:23). We cannot save ourselves, and we deserve the wrath of God (Rom. 2:5).

3. God's love for man. Yet despite our sinful ways, God has shown his great love for us (John 3:16; Rom. 5:8). In his mercy, he sent his Son, Jesus Christ, to die on the cross for us. On the cross Christ paid the full penalty for our sins and became the object of God's wrath (2 Cor. 5:21).

4. Man's response to God. If we confess and turn away from our sins and believe in Jesus Christ and the work he did for us on the cross, we can be saved (Mark 1:15; Rom. 10:9). If we possess faith to trust in God and the love he showed us through Jesus Christ, we are genuine Christians. We are justified—we receive forgiveness of our sins and are credited with Christ's righteousness, Jesus' life of perfect obedience (Rom. 3:24–27). In short, God restores our relationship with him and adopts us into his family because of his grace and not because of anything we do (Gal. 2:16; Titus 3:5).

God has shown us an amazing love, even though we are sinful and deserve his judgment. He sent his one and only Son to suffer greatly for us so that we can be forgiven and have Christ's righteousness counted as ours. He makes us new creatures with new hearts, and we can resist sin and mature as Christians. We can look forward to eternity in heaven with our glorious Lord.

So What?

At the end of this life, we will stand before God to be judged. He will either invite us into heaven to experience eternal joy or send us to hell, where we will experience his wrath for eternity.

My goal is that your heart would be stirred as you search your soul. My prayer for you is genuine salvation and assurance of salvation. My hope is that all false assurance will die. What a shame it would be if you thought you were saved, but in reality you were not!

If you have never confessed your sinfulness and placed your faith in the finished work of Jesus Christ, you can do so right now. If in the past you professed faith in Christ, but you haven't been living like a Christian, you can return to your

> ### THINK ABOUT IT
> Where will you spend eternity? This question is not designed to manipulate you by fear or guilt. My purpose in asking is the same as Charles Spurgeon's when he said:
>
> It is not my aim to introduce doubts and fears into your mind; no, but I do hope self-examination may help to drive them away. It is not security, but false security, which we would kill; not confidence, but false confidence, which we would overthrow; not peace, but false peace, which we would destroy.[11]
> —CHARLES SPURGEON

first love. God's love is great, and he may be drawing you to himself. In Mark 1:15 Jesus says, "Repent and believe the good news!" Romans 10:9 says, "If you confess with your mouth, 'Jesus is Lord,' and believe in your heart that God raised him from the dead, you will be saved." Please pause and consider what God is doing in your heart.

A Call to Action

False assurance is the most significant danger you face. Don't wrongly assume that you are a Christian just because of your parents or your environment. Salvation is by faith alone. Look at the fruit in your life to see whether you are a true Christian with a regenerated heart. Hearts that love God demonstrate love in consistent patterns of God-honoring thoughts, words, and actions. Hearts that do not love God demonstrate consistent patterns of ungodliness and worldliness. After close examination of your life, you should either have assurance of salvation or be challenged to repent and believe the message of the gospel.

Commit today to:

√ Carefully examine your life for evidence of salvation

√ If you are not saved, repent and believe the gospel

√ If you are saved, rejoice in the amazing love and kindness of God

Questions for Reflection and Discussion

1. What is false assurance of salvation?

2. Why do church kids tend to assume they are Christians, even if they are not? Why is this so dangerous?

3. How does a person become a Christian?

4. How can you tell if a person is a Christian? What kind of words and actions would you expect in the life of a true Christian?

5. Think of one person you know who you are confident is a Christian. How do you know?

6. Why is it important to consider the thoughts and motives behind your actions?

7. What did you learn about yourself through the 2 Corinthians 13 self-test?

8. Are you a Christian? How do you know?

9. Do your parents believe you are a Christian? Why?

10. What is the gospel? What does it mean to believe the gospel? Why did Jesus have to die on the cross?

Sing a New Song

"Before the Throne of God Above"[12]

Before the throne of God above
I have a strong and perfect plea
A great High Priest whose name is love
Who ever lives and pleads for me
My name is graven on His hands
My name is written on His heart
I know that while in heav'n He stands
No tongue can bid me thence depart
No tongue can bid me thence depart

When Satan tempts me to despair
And tells me of the guilt within
Upward I look and see Him there
Who made an end of all my sin
Because the sinless Savior died
My sinful soul is counted free
For God, the Just, is satisfied
To look on Him and pardon me
To look on Him and pardon me

Behold Him there! the risen Lamb
My perfect, spotless, Righteousness
The Great unchangeable I AM
The King of Glory and of Grace
One with Himself I cannot die
My soul is purchased by His blood
My life is hid with Christ on high
With Christ my Savior and my God
With Christ my Savior and my God

For more information on this song, go to www.growingupchristian.com.

But because of his great love for us, God, who is rich in mercy, made us alive with Christ even when we were dead in transgressions— it is by grace you have been saved.

—EPHESIANS 2:4–5

Lord, help me to

- grasp your great love for me.

- understand your holiness and my sinfulness.

- be amazed at your grace in saving me.

- appreciate your mercy in forgiving my sins.

3 UN-AMAZING GRACE

THE DANGER OF TAKING THE GRACE OF GOD FOR GRANTED

Rescued

On July 24, 2002, Randy Fogle went to work, expecting an ordinary day at the office. Never mind that his "office" is a dank subterranean labyrinth two hundred forty feet belowground, where the only light comes from flickering helmet lamps and a mistake can cost you your life. Randy had been a coal miner for twenty years, and he took such challenges in his stride. He had a reputation for toughness. Little did Randy know how his toughness was about to be tested to the limit.

His ordinary day's work was interrupted at about nine o'clock in the evening by a frantic voice crackling over his radio: "We hit water—get out!"

Randy's fellow miners had accidentally drilled through into an adjacent, flooded mine. The miners scrambled to escape, doubled over as they ran to avoid the low ceilings, as millions of gallons of water came swirling and gushing about their ankles. One team escaped. Randy's team did not. Cut off from their only exits by flooded corridors, the nine men found themselves trapped in a chamber only four feet deep and eighteen feet wide, filled nearly to the top with frigid 55-degree water.

These men had no shortage of strength or courage. They were fighters and survivors, hard men who faced danger on a daily basis. Randy had played football in high school. His brother recollected one time they'd been deer-hunting, and Randy had opted not to wear gloves even though it was five below zero. That's the kind of man he was. If anyone could find a way out of this mess, it was Randy and his fellow miners.

It didn't take long, however, for the terrible truth to become clear: Randy was helpless. As the minutes turned to hours, and the hours turned to days, the water wasn't receding. By day three, hypothermia and despair were setting in. There was nothing they could do, in and of their own strength. Resourcefulness and toughness weren't enough to save them. All they could do was hope and pray for rescue.

> **THINK ABOUT IT**
> You see, at just the right time, when we were still powerless, Christ died for the ungodly. (Rom. 5:6)
>
> As for you, you were dead in your transgressions and sins, in which you used to live. (Eph. 2:1–2)

Before our holy and righteous God, we are like the nine miners— helpless in our own abilities to save ourselves.

If salvation depended on our own efforts, we would not be able to accomplish it. Just as the miners totally depended on the team of experts to save their lives, we totally depend on God, through Jesus Christ, to save us from our sins. The Bible describes us as dead in our transgressions; if we are dead, how can we make ourselves alive again? We are helpless apart from God.

Can you imagine what it was like for the miners during those three days? What do you think went through their minds in the flooded mineshaft? They probably thought about what would happen to their families if they died and what they would enjoy again if they survived.

Mercifully, Randy and his companions didn't have to rely on their own resourcefulness. Their story made front-page headlines and gripped the nation. A rescue effort began immediately. Rescue workers, fellow miners, families, and friends worked and prayed day and night to save the lives of these brave men. It was slow, tiring, and difficult work, but nothing could shake their determination. They began by running a pipe into the subterranean chamber, pumping in hot air—a move that kept Randy and his friends alive. When the miners banged on the pipe, it gave their rescuers the first affirmation that they were still alive, and fueled their determination.

After seventy-seven hours of huddling in the frigid darkness, praying and thinking about his loved ones, Randy Fogle was finally raised to the surface in a yellow rescue cage. His eight companions followed. All survived with strong spirits and only minor injuries. Thanks to the devoted work of their rescuers, they had stared death in the face and come back to tell the story.

Now imagine their thoughts and reactions as they reached the surface alive. Imagine their words and expressions as they saw their loved ones, and those who were responsible for their rescue. Picture their expressions of utter thankfulness—a gratitude that transcends words. Can you hear the cheers and see their faces? Can you almost feel the embraces and taste their tears of joy?

Our response to God for his saving love should be no different. In fact, our gratitude should be even greater when we think of what he has saved us from.

Danger #2

As church kids, we can tend to view ourselves as being pretty good and not having sinned much—at least no really awful sins. Although we would never say it aloud, we are tempted to think that God got a pretty good person when he chose us to be part of his kingdom. We tend to erroneously see ourselves as having little sin and as having been forgiven of little sin. This way of thinking leads to a second danger church kids face: a lack of appreciation for the saving and forgiving grace of God.

Jerry Bridges defines grace as "God's free and unmerited favor shown to guilty sinners who deserve only judgment."[1] That is us—you and me, guilty sinners who deserve God's judgment. But do we really believe that we are guilty and deserve judgment? Our appreciation for the grace of God is directly proportional to our understanding of this simple fact.

> **THINK ABOUT IT**
> Grace never ignores the awful truth of our depravity. In fact, it emphasizes it. The worse we realize we are, the greater we realize God's grace is. [2]—RANDY ALCORN

Our amazement of our Savior depends primarily on our understanding of the huge separation between us and God and the great work he accomplished on the cross to bridge this great divide. A key to passionately loving God is in knowing that we have been forgiven of many sins.

Through Christ, we went from objects of God's wrath to objects of his love; from death to life; and from eternity in hell to eternity in heaven.

This is not a new message to us church kids; if we have heard it once, we may have heard it a thousand times. The problem arises when we don't truly believe we need to be saved from very many sins and therefore don't really think we need the gospel. We church kids are dead in our transgressions and are daily forgiven much, even though we aren't always mindful of it.

Take a moment to ask God to impress these truths on your heart, so that you will overflow with gratitude like the rescued miners. Then consider the following parable.

Take His Word for It

Amazement of God flows from a heart that deeply loves God. Jesus spoke about this love in Luke 7:36–50. As Jesus ate at a Pharisee's, a sinful woman came into the room. She washed Jesus' feet with her tears, dried them with her hair, and anointed Jesus with perfume. The Pharisee stared in shock. He couldn't believe that Jesus would even allow this sinful woman to be near him—let alone do these things to him.

Jesus responded by telling a simple and powerful story followed by a probing question: "Two men owed money to a certain moneylender. One owed him five hundred denarii, and the other fifty. Neither of them had the money to pay him back, so he canceled the debts of both. Now which of them will love him more?" (Luke 7:41–42).

The Pharisee correctly answered that the one with the larger debt would love the moneylender more. Jesus then explained that the sinful woman demonstrated such lavish love for him because she realized how much she had been forgiven. Those who realize that they have been forgiven much, love much, and those who think they have been forgiven little, love little (Luke 7:47).

Jesus told this story to challenge the perspective of the Pharisee and to commend the love demonstrated by this woman. In a simple story and one question, he both rebukes the self-righteous Pharisees and holds up the woman as an example of wholehearted devotion. Jesus' words apply just as much today as they did two thousand years ago, and they contain a valuable lesson for those of us who have grown up in Christian homes.

> **THINK ABOUT IT**
> We were by nature objects of wrath. But because of his great love for us, God, who is rich in mercy, made us alive with Christ even when we were dead in transgressions—it is by grace you have been saved. (Eph. 2:3–5)

Jesus clearly connects our appreciation of the forgiveness of God with our love for him. When we realize Christ died on the cross for each of our sins, we will love him much. When we understand that Jesus experienced the wrath of God in our place, we will love him much. When we realize that we have been credited with the righteousness of Christ when nothing in us is worthy, we will love him much. And when we consider that God will accept us into heaven for eternity because of this finished work of Jesus Christ, we will love him much.

Jesus also connects our lack of understanding of the forgiveness of God with loving him little. If we fail to see the depth of our sinfulness or we do not think we have much to be forgiven, we will love him little.

51

Saving and Forgiving Grace

I have heard the testimonies of many people who did not grow up in a Christian home. You know the type of people I am talking about: tears falling from their eyes as they recount the life of drugs and alcohol that Jesus saved them from when they were 22 or 23, or jumping up and down with joy and shouts of praise to God for saving them from a life of sexual sin. When I hear testimonies like these, I realize that as church kids we have a distinctly different experience of the saving and forgiving grace of God in our lives.

I became a Christian a few weeks before my fourth birthday. My first memory is kneeling beside my bed professing Jesus as my Savior. Because I do not recall anything prior to that day, I do not remember a drastic life change once I became a Christian. I can erroneously think that salvation did not make any difference in my life because I do not remember being unsaved. As a result, I am tempted to be un-amazed at the saving grace of God.

Contrast my salvation experience with the stories of individuals whom God saved in their twenties. They remember a specific change in their goals, priorities, desires, and lives as a result of their conversion. They can describe a time when Christ made a significant difference in their lives, and they have a good idea of what their lives would be like if God had never saved them.

The fact is, you and I have just as great a reason to have tears in our eyes when we recount our testimony. Although I have never committed the exact types of sins often described by people saved later in life, I am just as sinful. Yet I tend to have a wrong view of my sin. I am inclined to think that I have not sinned very much. But how many sins have I committed in my lifetime? While I know I have committed an abundance of sins in my words and actions, I can also quickly list for you a vast amount of sins that I commit in my thoughts. When I take an honest look at myself, I see sins of anger, deceit, lust, arrogance, coveting, impatience, complaining, resisting authority, disrespecting my parents, critically judging others, and fearing the opinion of others—just to name a few. I tend to grow more mindful of the sin in my heart as I walk daily with the Lord. The truth is I am naturally sinful and frequently sin. But when I realize that I have been forgiven for each and every one of these sins, I stand amazed by God's glorious forgiving grace in my life.

Actually, when we remember all that God has protected us from, and everything he has given us in being raised in Christian environments, we have even more reason to express tears of gratitude when we share our testimonies.

A Look in the Mirror

Thankfully, we can grow in appreciation of God's grace. As we consider the blessings of knowing God from a young age and correctly see our sinfulness, our amazement at the grace of God will increase.

Church kids should be some of the most appreciative people on the earth. God has shown us amazing grace not only in saving us, but also in saving us at such a young age and placing us in Christian homes where we can be protected, trained, and discipled. God has shown us immense favor every day of our lives. We truly do owe him everything!

> **THINK ABOUT IT**
> If only we could see our situation clearly—even for a moment. We deserve expulsion; He gives us a diploma. We deserved the electric chair; He gives us a parade. Anything less than overwhelming gratitude should be unthinkable. He owes us nothing. We owe Him everything.[3] —RANDY ALCORN

Harden not your hearts to the hearing of the good news over and over again from a young age, but ask God to give you a fresh appreciation and understanding of all that he has done for you.

How can we tell if we appreciate the grace of God in our lives? How can we know if we are amazed at God? Let's take a few moments to evaluate ourselves.

SELF-EVALUATION

Read the following statements, and rate yourself on a scale of 1 to 10. *10 means that you strongly agree and 1 means that you strongly disagree.*

___ 1. I am extremely grateful that God has saved me.

___ 2. I regularly think of what my life would be like if God had not saved me.

___ 3. When I look at my life, I see a lot of sin.

___ 4. I am often amazed that God forgives me, even when I repeatedly sin.

___ 5. When I pray, I frequently thank God for forgiving my sins.

___ 6. I love to worship God and express my love for him in song.

___ 7. I really enjoy talking with others about God.

___ 8. I look for opportunities to share my faith with others.

___ 9. I am extremely excited about spending eternity in heaven.

___10. I regularly thank God for saving me from eternity in hell.

Take a minute to look over your ratings. How would you evaluate yourself overall? Do you seem to appreciate the saving and forgiving grace of God in your life?

Tips for Growth

What can we do if we want to grow in our appreciation for the grace of God? Here are seven tips to consider:

1. Pray. Growth starts with God, and it is essential that we start by asking him for help (Matt. 7:7–8). We need his help to more clearly understand his character as opposed to our sinfulness. We need his help to gain a greater appreciation for our salvation. We need his help to grasp the undeserved kindness he shows us in repeatedly forgiving our sins—day after day, week after week, year after year. And we need his help to see the many blessings that surround us.

Amazingly, he is eager to answer our prayers!

2. Study the holiness of God. The more we learn about God's holiness (Lev. 19:2)—his separateness—the more we will appreciate his saving and forgiving grace. He is holy and blameless and can have nothing to do with the wicked and the sinful. Without the substitutionary work of Jesus Christ on the cross, God could have nothing to do with sinful man. It is hard to grasp how far above us God is.

We need to pick up our Bibles and study the holiness of God. We can also read great works by theologians such as Wayne Grudem,[4] J. C. Ryle,[5] and J. I. Packer.[6]

THINK ABOUT IT

In comparing himself to a child molester and murderer named Dodd, Randy Alcorn uses a radical illustration to explain the difference between sinful man and a holy God. I pray that we come to know God's holiness as deeply as Alcorn does.

I'd imagined the distance between Dodd and me as the difference between the South and North Poles. But when you consider God's viewpoint from light-years away, that distance is negligible. In my standing before a holy God apart from Christ . . . I am Dodd. . . . Unless we come to grips with the fact that we're of precisely the same stock—fallen humanity—as Dodd and Hitler and Stalin, we'll never appreciate Christ's grace.[7]—RANDY ALCORN

3. See your sinfulness in light of God's holiness. To grow in our appreciation for the grace of God, we need to have an accurate view of our natural sinfulness and its offense to our holy God. Again, we can study this more in depth by reading the Bible and books by theologians such as John Owen[8] and Chris Lungaard.[9]

4. Learn more about God's wrath—his just response to sin. After seeking to understand God's holiness and our sinful nature, we need to examine God's just response to sin. If we desire to increase our appreciation for the grace of God, we must understand the nature and the object of his wrath.

This is a topic we often wish to avoid because it makes us feel uncomfortable, but the wrath of God is a reality of the Christian faith. Temporary discomfort can be good if we learn how much God hates sin. In the end we will learn to hate it, too.

5. Think deeply and often about Jesus' death on the cross. When we understand the significance of Jesus' death on the cross, we will grow in our appreciation of the grace of God. Jesus experienced a brutal death on our behalf. In addition to the great physical pain, he experienced the guilt of our sin, the wrath of God, and separation from God—all of which he had never before known. Motivated by a deep love for us all, he bore the consequences of our sin.

We need to read about Jesus' death on the cross. We need to faithfully remind ourselves by thinking and praying about it. We must make sure that we do not grow so familiar with the cross that we forget that it was the moment when Christ bridged the huge divide between God and us. What amazing love! What amazing grace!

6. Study the doctrine of justification—forgiven and declared righteous. The more we understand about our salvation, the more amazed we will be at God's love and kindness toward us. When we place our faith in the finished work of Jesus Christ on the cross, God justifies us. He declares us not guilty and also credits us with the righteousness of Christ. We aren't just forgiven of all our sins; he sees us the same way he sees his Son—perfectly righteous. Wow! What kindness!

7. Sing great songs that focus on the grace of God. Worshipful songs and hymns are powerful tools that God gives us to praise him and ingrain truths in our hearts. We need to sing songs that focus on the cross, the forgiveness of God, and the grace of God. The Holy Spirit will use them to warm our hearts and help us grow in our appreciation for the grace of God. We need to sing these songs all day, around our houses or in our cars.[10]

A Call to Action

Recognize your situation. As a church kid, you face the danger of failing to appreciate the grace of God in your life. Guard against growing familiar with your salvation. Resist the temptation to wrongly view your sin as little. Instead, glory in your salvation and view each and every one of your sins as offensive to your holy God.

Commit today to:

√ Ask God to increase your amazement of his saving and forgiving grace
√ Learn more about the holiness of God
√ Comprehend your sinful nature
√ Glory in your salvation

Questions for Reflection and Discussion

1. What is *grace*? What is forgiving grace? What is saving grace?

2. What does it mean to be amazed at the grace of God in your life?

3. Who is one person you know who is clearly amazed at the grace of God in his or her life? How do you see it evidenced in that person's life?

4. Why do church kids tend to lack an appreciation for the grace of God? Why is this dangerous?

5. How do individuals who become Christians as adults tend to differ from those who were saved at a young age? Why are they different?

6. What did you learn about yourself from your self-evaluation? Would you describe yourself as amazed or un-amazed at the grace of God? Why or why not?

7. What advice would you give someone who wants to grow in amazement of God's grace in his or her life?

8. Consider the seven tips for growing in your appreciation for the grace of God. Which one do you already do well? Which one do you most need to concentrate on in the next few months?

9. How should someone pray if he or she wants to grow in amazement of the grace of God in his or her life?

Sing a New Song

"I Will Glory in My Redeemer"[11]

I will glory in my Redeemer
Whose priceless blood has ransomed me
Mine was the sin that drove the bitter nails
And hung Him on that judgment tree
I will glory in my Redeemer
Who crushed the power of sin and death
My only Savior before the Holy Judge
The lamb who is my righteousness
The lamb who is my righteousness

I will glory in my Redeemer
My life He bought, my love He owns
I have no longing for another
I'm satisfied in Him alone
I will glory in my Redeemer
His faithfulness my standing place
Though foes are mighty and rush upon me
My feet are firm held by His grace
My feet are firm held by His grace

I will glory in my Redeemer
Who carries me on eagle's wings
He crowns my life with lovingkindness
His triumph song I'll ever sing
I will glory in my Redeemer
Who waits for me at gates of gold
And when he calls me it will be paradise
His face forever to behold
His face forever to behold

For more information on this song, go to www.growingupchristian.com.

Do not love the world or anything in the world. If anyone loves the world, the love of the Father is not in him. For everything in the world—the cravings of sinful man, the lust of his eyes and the boasting of what he has and does—comes not from the Father but from the world. The world and its desires pass away, but the man who does the will of God lives forever.

—1 John 2:15–17

Lord, help me to

- love you above all else.

- see how I love the world and things of the world.

- recognize and reject the lies of the world.

- impact this culture for your glory.

4 THE COST OF COMPROMISE

THE DANGER OF LOVING THE WORLD

Change

Curt was sitting on a brick flowerbed sidewall outside the mall, counting a wad of crumpled bills, when he saw the last person in the world he'd ever expected to see again. He stuffed the cash into his jacket and looked for a place to slip off to, but Bo had already seen him.

Bo waved. He wore a delighted grin. "Curt? Man, I haven't seen you in months. How you been?"

"Good," Curt managed, adding nothing to encourage further conversation.

Bo sat down beside him and clapped him on the shoulder. "I can't believe I ran into you like this, because I've been wanting to talk to you. I was thinking about you just the other day, in fact. You remember that chapel message you gave at the beginning of our senior year? The one about the fear of God?"

"Yeah." Curt's throat had gone dry.

"Well, God really used that message in my life. I was trying to figure a lot of things out on my own, about myself and what I want from life, but your message spoke to me about God's wisdom. After that message I just let go and started trusting him, and life has just been good since then, you know? It's hard to put into words, but I just wanted to say thanks, man. You always had so much good insight to share. I'm glad there are godly guys like you out there."

"Thanks, Bo," Curt muttered.

Bo suddenly checked his watch. "Hey, man, I've got to get to work. Come see me sometime; I work at Victor's Sports Locker. It was great seeing you!"

"Yeah, sure."

Bo clapped him on the shoulder again, flashed him a final grin, then rushed into the mall.

"*I'm glad there are godly guys like you out there,*" a voice piped from behind him in a mocking, girlish tone. Jared plopped down where Bo had been sitting and laughed. "You're just full of surprises, Curt."

"Shut up. I haven't seen that guy in like two years. Just give me my stuff, and let's get out of here." Curt slapped his cash into Jared's palm.

Jared chuckled and shook his head as he counted the bills. "Godly guy. Huh. That explains why you keep telling me you're gonna quit."

"Yeah, well, maybe next week. Yesterday I lost my job, and my dad says I can't live in the house if I keep things up with my girlfriend. I just want a few joints to get me through the week. Then I'm done."

"Hey, no need to make excuses to me. I'll take your money anytime. You just keep talking like you're gonna quit, that's all. More power to you if you do. I'm still surprised you lasted as long as you did before trying this stuff. You were always that guy at the parties holding out, saying no." Jared chuckled. "I guess it was just a matter of time."

Curt flushed with anger. Those words hit too close to home. "Just give me the bag!"

"Yeah, man, sorry. Here. I'm sure I'll probably see you here next week." Jared pressed the small bundle of weed into Curt's hand, and then he was gone.

In but Not Of

How did Curt go from being a spiritual leader to a drug user? He did it the same way that each of us changes—one choice at a time. Curt didn't suddenly wake up a user one day. His slide started when he began to socialize with a rough crowd, then hang out with them more regularly, then attend parties where drug use was commonplace. Ultimately he gave in to the pressure from his new friends, and tried his first joint. Before long, he was smoking marijuana almost every day.

It is a challenge for a Christian to live in the world but not be worldly. We watch celebrities, listen to music, and see movies, and we are drawn to what we observe. People appear to be having fun, and we want to have fun, too. We think we know the dangers of the world, and we assume we can gain the *benefits* of the world while avoiding its *pitfalls*. We naively believe that a little bit of the world won't harm us.

It's easy to spot the flagrant sins promoted in the world, such as sex outside of marriage, pornography, homosexuality, and abortion. But we often fail to pick up on the subtle lies in the TV shows we watch, the magazines we read, and the music we listen to. We nibble at the table of the world and either miss or minimize its effect on our lives.

> **THINK ABOUT IT**
> The greatest enemy of hunger for God is not poison but apple pie. It is not the banquet of the wicked that dulls our appetite for heaven, but endless nibbling at the table of the world. It is not the X-rated video, but the prime-time dribble of triviality we drink in every night. . . . For when these replace an appetite for God himself, the idolatry is scarcely recognizable, and almost incurable. [1]—JOHN PIPER

Danger #3

This brings us to the third dangerous tendency of church kids: loving the world. While we are seeking to find satisfaction in the things of this world, our lives begin to gradually model the lifestyles and values of the world. One decision at a time—sometimes without even realizing it—we gradually begin to think, speak, and act like the world around us.

Have you ever had a classmate who has grown two or three inches over the summer? If you haven't seen him for a few months, you will immediately notice the change the first time you see him. But if you have hung out with him most of the summer, you may not even notice his growth. Typically, we don't see daily physical change. The change in our hearts due to loving the world is even more subtle.

We think we are the same every day, but we fail to see small changes in our values due to the parties we attend, the books we read, and the movies we watch. We think a little worldliness won't hurt us, but little by little we change. And slight changes over time add up to huge change in our lives.

Church kids seem to be particularly attracted to the things of the world. We can look over the fence to the grass of the world and think it is greener. Before long we're tasting samples of what we find, oblivious to the rotting effect those poisoned values have in our lives.

> ## THINK ABOUT IT
>
> In C. S. Lewis's masterful work *The Screwtape Letters*—a book containing letters from Screwtape, an experienced demon, to his nephew Wormwood, a novice demon—Lewis highlights the danger of steady, gradual change:
>
> Indeed the safest road to Hell is the gradual one—the gentle slope, soft underfoot, without sudden turnings, without milestones, without signposts.[2]—Screwtape

Before going any further, let me make you aware of two extreme responses that I am *not* promoting: (1) completely withdrawing from the world, or (2) thinking that the world is nothing to worry about. God doesn't call us to completely flee from the world by throwing out our TVs, never attending movies, destroying our CD players, and moving to remote cabins in the woods. But he does call us to use discernment in evaluating the content of each of these things. My prayer for you is like Paul's prayer for the Philippians: "that your love may abound more and more in knowledge and depth of insight, so that you may be able to discern what is best and may be pure and blameless until the day of Christ" (Phil. 1:9–10).

God has given us knowledge of himself, what pleases him, and what is good and bad for us as his children. We need to use this knowledge to evaluate the things of the world. We cannot bury our heads in the sand and think of the world as good or even neutral. The purpose of this chapter is to raise our awareness of the danger of loving the world and provide tools to help navigate this danger so we can live in the world but not be worldly.

Take His Word for It

What's the Big Deal?

The passage in 1 John 2:15–17 provides four points to consider:

1. God commands us to not love the world or the things of the world. Therefore, loving either is direct disobedience to God.
2. Loving God and loving the world are opposites and cannot be done at the same time.
3. The values of the world contradict the standards of God. Man has sinful cravings, and God cannot sin; man lusts with his eyes, and God is holy; man is prideful, and God opposes the proud.
4. Don't be fooled. There is something much better than the temporary pleasures of the world—God. When we love him and obey him, we can look forward to eternity in heaven with him.

> **THINK ABOUT IT**
> Let's start by examining why loving the world is so dangerous:
>
> Do not love the world or anything in the world. If anyone loves the world, the love of the Father is not in him. For everything in the world—the cravings of sinful man, the lust of his eyes and the boasting of what he has and does—comes not from the Father but from the world. The world and its desires pass away, but the man who does the will of God lives forever. (1 John 2:15–17)

We must understand that loving the world and the things of the world is the complete opposite of loving God. James 4:4 again makes this clear: "don't you know that friendship with the world is hatred toward God?" Scripture describes us as waging war with the world

(2 Cor. 10:3–5). And Jesus recognized the danger that his disciples faced when he prayed, "My prayer is not that you take them out of the world but that you protect them from the evil one" (John 17:15).

Take God's Word for it. The world is a powerful enemy that we face every day. Admit the danger, watch out for it, and flee from it or fight it.

We Often Miss It

So often we miss the seriousness of the world's influence. That's when loving the world is particularly dangerous. Like a cracking and eroding foundation of a house, our Christian worldview can splinter and decay for years without being detected as we fall in love with the world. When the problem is finally detected, the damage is severe. In a house, a weak and crumbling foundation will damage almost every aspect of the structure. In a person, loving the world will seriously affect friendships, decisions, thought life, conscience, passion for God, and much more.

What effect is the world having on you? Do you see how it brings subtle and relentless pressure on you? Do you see how it creeps up on you little by little? Or are you missing it?

> **THINK ABOUT IT**
>
> The world . . . is characterized by the subtle and relentless pressure it brings to bear upon us to conform to its values and practices. It creeps up on us little by little. What was once unthinkable becomes thinkable, then doable, and finally acceptable to society at large. Sin becomes respectable, and so Christians finally embrace it. It is my perception that Christians are no more than five to ten years behind the world in embracing most sinful practices. [3]
> —JERRY BRIDGES

A Look in the Mirror

What Can I Get Away With?

At 4:28 p.m. Tim was in position, waiting on his bed with his telephone in hand. Exactly two minutes later it rang, making Tim jump even though he'd known the call was coming. He answered after the first ring, before his mom would have a chance to pick up the phone downstairs.

"Hello?" Tim's heart was pounding.

"Hey, Tim!"

"Crystal! You're exactly on time. What's up?"

He got comfortable on the bed and listened as Crystal proceeded to tell him about her day. His pulse slowly returned to normal. It was ridiculous getting so worked up about this, he knew, but Crystal wasn't a Christian and he knew his parents wouldn't approve of their blossoming interest in each other. They'd been hanging out for a month now at school, but had started calling each other only recently. Tim tried his hardest to keep the calls secret. Calling Crystal was usually easy to conceal, but she liked to call him as well, and he didn't want her to think he was afraid of his parents. He tried to save face by allowing Crystal to call, but suggesting times when he knew he could answer the phone before his parents or sister did. So far, so good.

They talked briefly and made arrangements to meet in the library in the morning before school; then Crystal had to go. A little while later Tim's mom poked her head into his room. "Who called?" she asked.

"It was Sam," Tim quickly lied.

"Really? I picked up the phone after it rang, but you'd already answered it. I could have sworn you were talking to a girl."

Dead silence filled the air. Tim knew he'd been caught in a lie. They stood there looking at each other in awkward silence, before his mom closed the door and went back downstairs.

Tim jumped off the bed and started pacing around his room, trying to forecast how bad the fallout would be. His mom would tell his dad when he got home from work. Dad would ask questions. They didn't know about Crystal, but they would find out, and they would forbid him to date her. They also might ground him for keeping the relationship a secret.

He grimaced at how embarrassing it would be to break up with Crystal like this. After all, he was in high school now. He didn't want to lose her, either. She was cute and popular, and a lot of fun.

It was time for damage control. Tim went downstairs and found his mom.

"Mom, I lied to you about Sam. I'm sorry. I haven't been totally honest with you about some things. Can I talk about this with you and Dad tonight?" Tim was impressed with his own words. He was pouring it on smooth, and his mother was buying it. He would tell his parents just enough to get them off his back. He would tell them that Crystal was working with him on a group project at school, and that was the extent of their relationship. He'd say that he'd lied about the call because, even though she wasn't a Christian, he felt some attraction to her and wasn't sure how to cope with those feelings. If they bought that story, he'd be free and clear. They'd never have to know how substantial his relationship with Crystal really was. He'd just have to be more careful in the future.

Can you relate to Tim? Have you ever lied to your parents to hide something from them? Concealing things from your parents is a sign of a problem in your heart. In particular, hiding worldliness from your parents indicates a growing love for the world, which is a growing problem. Is there anything, even something small, that you are keeping from your parents?

If you have godly parents, they can be your greatest assets in resisting worldliness. Keeping open and honest lines of communication with them regarding your questions and temptations about things of the world can be the very thing that keeps you from sliding down this slippery slope. Don't be afraid to talk with them. Take advantage of their wisdom and what they know about the Enemy's methods of deceit. If you don't have believing parents who can fulfill this role, continue to honor and respect them, but also seek out mentorship from adult believers in your church or community, such as pastors or youth-group leaders.

We have to think carefully about how the world influences us right now through television, music, movies, the Internet, and friendships. Take a few moments to ask yourself the following questions:

WHAT INFLUENCES YOU?

Briefly answer each question.

1. What are your favorite TV shows, movies, and bands?
2. What values do they promote?
3. How do their values compare to the Word of God?
4. Do you critically evaluate TV shows or music CDs? How?
5. Is there anything you refuse to watch or listen to? Why?
6. What types of Internet sites do you tend to visit?
7. How do you determine whether a site is worth exploring?
8. Do you think your entertainment habits please God?
9. What qualities do you look for in friends?
10. Do you see these qualities in your current friends?
11. Do your friends influence you toward godliness or worldliness?

What is your overall assessment of yourself? What is the dominant influence in your life: God or the world? How would your parents or mature Christian friends rate you in these same areas?

What Should We Do?

We must daily resist the world and battle the urge to love the world. This comes from recognizing our situation, watching, analyzing, resisting, and repenting.

1. Recognizing our situation. At the end of a long day, we often plop down on the couch and watch TV. Flipping through the sixty channels, we settle on a sitcom. The plot develops, and the funny lines come one after another. We lean back and relax, joining the studio audience in laughter, not even noticing our dangerous situation.

> **THINK ABOUT IT**
> The subtle influence of that mighty enemy [the world] must be daily resisted, and without a daily battle can never be overcome.[4]
> —J. C. RYLE

With pretty much any form of entertainment (TV, movies, videos, music, magazines, books, and the Internet), we tend to relax and let our guard down at the precise moment that we should be preparing to wage war. Sometimes these types of entertainment can be good, but so often they contradict a truth or standard of Scripture. We must recognize that the world around us is non-Christian and does affect us, and we need to admit that we are naturally attracted to it. Then we will be ready to see its methods and reject its lies.

2. Watching. Having recognized our situation, when we lie on the couch to watch TV, we will be on guard for the lure of the world. When we hit the power button on the remote, we must begin to watch out for the lies.

THINK ABOUT IT

We need to develop what Jerry Bridges calls the "discipline of watching":

We need to be watchful in the little things of everyday life, the little issues that seem so unimportant—the little lie, the little bit of pride, the little lustful glance, or the little bit of gossip . . . the truth is, it is in the minutiae of life where most of us live day after day. We seldom have to say no to an outright temptation to adultery. We often have to say no to the temptation to the lustful look or thought. And as some unknown person has said, "He that despises little things shall fall little by little." [5]
—Jerry Bridges

It's true. We need to be on the lookout for the "little things," so that we will be prepared to say no to the more obvious sins. Watching is the first step in avoiding or battling any sin, especially worldliness.

Have you developed the discipline of watching?

---

3. Analyzing. As long as we live on this earth, we will never be able to completely eliminate the influence of the world. We need to avoid temptations whenever possible and be prepared for the temptations that are inevitable. When we cannot flee from evil, we must learn to reject evil. When we cannot flee from the influences of the world, we must learn to analyze its methods and message so we can reject anything contrary to the standards of God.

Let's consider TV. As you sit down to watch TV, count the minutes. How long until you hear the first swear word, how long before the first sexual joke, how long until a violent act takes place, or how long until a child shows clear disrespect to a parent? Probably not too long! Start watching for these things, and you will be amazed. Analyze the humor in a show. Often it centers on foul language, sexuality, or disrespect or rebellion, and the limit is always being pushed.

Humor can be a means by which the world subtly influences us. When we laugh at something, we tend to accept it and think it is okay, good, or appropriate. Slowly, over time, we begin to accept things that we rejected earlier. We begin to ignore our moral beliefs, we compromise with the world, and we sin—first in thought and later in word and deed. The next time you watch a sitcom, analyze what you're really laughing at. You probably won't laugh as much anymore—you'll probably turn the TV off.

Entertainers can also influence our appearance. We will often buy the style of clothes that we see celebrities wear. We'll change our hairstyles to match those of actors. Observe your classmates. They'll be wearing the latest trends in clothing found on television or in the movies. The influence of our culture can be so subtle. The reality is that we can honor or dishonor God in the way we dress, the way we talk, and the way we think. We need to intend to please God in all we do.

How does the world influence us? How does it affect our values and goals? Don't be deceived; the world has a message to communicate—goals to accomplish—both directly and indirectly.

THINK ABOUT IT

Our Morals and Personal Beliefs

Truth

What the World Says	What God Says
You cannot know what is true. Truth is relative. There is no absolute truth.	God is truth. His Word is the standard for truth. (Ps. 119:142, 151, 160)
Lying is sometimes good or best. White lies are okay.	God hates lying. (Prov. 6:17)

Romantic Relationships

You need a boyfriend or a girlfriend. You will find popularity and fulfillment through a romantic relationship.	You will find fulfillment in God alone. (Ps. 16:11) God created marriage to bless us.
Sex outside of marriage is okay, and everyone does it.	God has designed sex for a husband and wife. Outside of marriage, it is sin. (Eph. 5:3)

Language

You must tolerate contradictory views; don't speak against the opinions of others.	Fear God and not man. (Ps. 111:10; Prov. 29:25; Matt. 10:28)
It's only words.	We will give an account for every word we speak. (Matt. 12:36)
You have freedom of speech.	Speak only words that are helpful. (Eph. 4:29)
Swearing is okay. Vulgar language can be funny.	Do not swear. Speak only words that build others up. (Eph. 4:29)

Dress

You have to have the latest fashions. Your appearance is what really matters.	In whatever you do, do it for the glory of God. (1 Cor. 10:31) Man looks at outward appearance, but God looks at the heart. (1 Sam. 16:7)
You must dress provocatively in order to attract a boyfriend or girlfriend.	Women are to dress modestly. (1 Tim. 2:9) Don't do anything out of vain conceit. (Phil. 2:3)

Pride

Take pride in yourself and your talents.	God is the source of all your talents. (James 1:17)
You need to think highly of yourself to succeed in life.	Think lowly of yourself. Be humble, and God will exalt you. (1 Peter 5:5)
You can do anything you set your mind to.	You can do all things through Christ who strengthens you. (Phil. 4:13)
Promote your strengths, and you will get promoted.	Boast in the Lord. (2 Cor. 10:17)

Our Goals in Life

Education

Go to a prestigious school.	Love God with your mind. (Matt. 22:37) Trust in him, and he will direct your paths. (Prov. 3:5–6)
Seek to major in a field in which you can get an impressive job.	In whatever you do, do it for the glory of God. (1 Cor. 10:31)

Career

Seek a career that will get you a lot of money.	The love of money is the root of all kinds of evil. (1 Tim. 6:10)
Seek positions of power, leadership, and influence.	Serve others. Biblical greatness requires a humble heart. (Matt. 18:3–4)

View of Self

Do what is in your best interest.	Consider others better than yourself. (Phil. 2:3)
Think of yourself first.	Treat others the way you wish to be treated. (Luke 6:31)
	Look to the interests of others. (Phil. 2:4)

Our View of Authority
(e.g., Parents, Pastors, Teachers, and Civil Leaders)

Rebellion

Stick up for your rights. Fight for your rights.	Consider it pure joy when you face trials. (James 1:2–4)
Question authority.	Obey your leaders and submit to their authority. (Heb. 13:17)
Not all rules apply to you.	God has established the authority in our lives. (Rom. 13:1)

Resistance

Resist opening up to authority. Resist being honest with authority.	Honor and obey parents. (Eph. 6:1–3) Submit to civil authority. (Rom. 13:1–4)
Resist showing your weaknesses to authority.	God gives grace and help to the humble. (1 Peter 5:5)

Respect

Respect athletic, music, and movie stars. It is okay to disrespect parents, teachers, and spiritual leaders.	Respect those who work hard among you and are over you in the Lord. Hold them in the highest regard. (1 Thess. 5:12–13)
Respect those who respect you. Respect those who treat you well.	Love your enemies and pray for those who persecute you. (Matt. 5:44)
Treat others as they treat you.	Treat others the way you wish to be treated. (Luke 6:31)

4. Repenting. Have you identified any area in which you love the world or the things of the world? Have you seen areas of compromise in your life? If you have, God calls you to repent.

Repentance means turning from our sins to God. We need to identify the sin, confess it to God, put off the sinful practices, and put on godly practices. In this process we will feel remorse and experience the love and forgiveness of God.[6]

Finally, rejoice. Yes, rejoice! God's grace is amazing. His love for us is unmatched. His forgiveness is real and sweet.

A Call to Action

Be aware of the danger of loving the world. Compromise in this area is often subtle, but it has extreme consequences. Loving the world is sin against God and will greatly affect your love and passion for God.

Commit today to:
- √ Love God and not love the world
- √ Identify and repent of any way you have loved the world
- √ Not seek pleasure in the things of the world
- √ Recognize and reject the message and influence of the world
- √ Impact the world around you for Christ

Questions for Reflection and Discussion

1. What does it mean to love the world?
2. What does John Piper mean by "endless nibbling at the table of the world"?
3. Why is loving the world a particular danger that church kids face?
4. What is wrong with loving the world?
5. Why is hiding your love for the world from your parents a dangerous sign?
6. What are the key ways you are influenced by the world? How do music, TV, movies, and friendships influence you?
7. How effectively do you evaluate television, movies, music, the Internet, and friendships?
8. What is the discipline of watching? How does someone develop this discipline?
9. What is one way you can love the world less in the next month?
10. What is one way you can love God more in the next month?
11. How can your parents, pastor, and friends help you in loving the world less and loving God more?

Sing a New Song

"You Have Captured Me"[8]

I have tasted of a love
Sweeter than the honeycomb
And I have heard the symphony
Of Your whisper in my soul
But I am ruined for this world
For none compares with You my Lord

Chorus
For You have captured me
Completely captured me
And I'm consumed
With You and only You Jesus

There's a grace I can't resist
Loving arms are drawing me
And there's a beauty far beyond
What eyes of flesh could ever see
For I've beheld with trembling joy
The sight of Calvary's Scarlet Rose

For more information on this song, go to www.growingupchristian.com.

PART **2** THINKING BIBLICALLY

This is the one I esteem: he who is humble and contrite in spirit, and trembles at my word.

—ISAIAH 66:2

Lord, help me to

- understand what it means to be humble.

- see any pride in my life.

- hate self-righteousness.

- grow in humility.

5 BIBLICAL GREATNESS

CULTIVATING A HUMBLE HEART

Football and Life

Bill Yoast was a man whose fierce determination and stubborn pride had won him game after game coaching the T. C. Williams High School football team. So it came as a shock when, in the early 1970s at the newly racially integrated school, this respected white leader was told that a black man had been hired to replace him as head coach and offensive coordinator for the Titans. Yoast's only consolation was that he would stay on as defensive coordinator. Though he was far from pleased, he smugly insisted that the new coach wouldn't cut it and that he would be back in the head coach's job next season.

Yoast's rival was named Herman Boone, and he's played by Denzel Washington in the movie *Remember the Titans*. You might remember it as a movie about football, but it's really a story about racial prejudice and reconciliation. The focus of the movie is the titanic clash of wills between Boone and Yoast. Throughout the season the Titans win game after game, but the tension between the coaches keeps building, undermining each victory and threatening to tear the team apart. The players continue to succeed in spite of their coaches, whose stubborn pride is leading the team toward disaster.

The conflict comes into dramatic focus at the movie's climax, as the Titans battle Marshall High School in the state championship game. The Titans are struggling, particularly with their defense. By halftime they're down 0 to 7, and the way they've been playing, it's a miracle they're even doing that well. Boone and Yoast have locked horns the entire game, resulting in a divided team and disjointed strategy. Their pride is about to cost the Titans the state title.

Then, at the halftime break, the movie reaches its turning point. Yoast's ten-year-old daughter speaks the movie's simplest, yet most profound wisdom: "Coach, now isn't the time to be proud." This admonition gives Yoast pause. He realizes he's standing at a crossroads, not just in this game, but in his life. He has a decision to make.

Moved by his daughter's rebuke, Yoast heads into the locker room and stands in front of the entire team. To their great shock, he tells Boone, "I sure could use your help." It's an expression of humility that the Titans have never seen from Yoast.

The game hinges on this statement. Humility opens the door to help, and Boone responds honorably. He immediately takes over and decides to use his best players to play both offense and defense in the second half. Mounting a comeback, the Titans find themselves late in the fourth quarter in a position to win the game.

Yoast's humility sets a precedent for the rest of the team. At the start of the second half, a white player gives up his defensive cornerback position to a black teammate who he knows is better. Then, just before the last play of the game, Yoast suggests that Coach Boone call a reverse play. Boone listens and calls the play, and the result is a touchdown and a state championship.

As the players and fans erupt in frenzied celebration, the coaches embrace. Yoast says to Boone, "I know football . . . what you did with these boys . . . you're the right man for the job." Boone responds, "You're hall of fame in my book."

80

Both coaches had to make decisions, when their pride or humility determined the fate of the entire team. For much of the movie they chose the path of pride, and the result was division, controversy, and mean-spiritedness. By the end of the movie the coaches had learned to walk a different path. They made a choice to listen to each other, and the ensuing camaraderie and teamwork enabled the Titans to win the state championship.[1]

Robert Frost's poem *The Road Not Taken* is an apt metaphor for the crossroads at which we often find ourselves in life. What might seem a small choice at the time can set us upon an entire journey. As you read this poem, imagine yourself standing at this fork. Consider the two diverging roads to be the path of humility and the path of pride.

"The Road Not Taken"
by Robert Frost

Two roads diverged in a yellow wood,
And sorry I could not travel both
And be one traveler, long I stood
And looked down one as far as I could
To where it bent in the undergrowth;

Then took the other, as just as fair,
And having perhaps the better claim,
Because it was grassy and wanted wear;
Though as for that the passing there
Had worn them really about the same,

And both that morning equally lay
In leaves no step had trodden black.
Oh, I kept the first for another day!
Yet knowing how way leads on to way,
I doubted if I should ever come back.

I shall be telling this with a sigh
Somewhere ages and ages hence:
Two roads diverged in a wood, and I—

I took the one less traveled by,
And that has made all the difference.

The little decisions we make each day add up over time to set the course of our lives. In this chapter, we will look at a decision we face countless times each day: whether to follow the path of humility or the path of pride. These paths lead in radically different directions, affecting every aspect of our lives. The decisions we make each day—pursuing pride or humility—will truly make all the difference in our Christian walk.

Our Tendency

The Pharisee in Luke 18:9–14 represented self-righteous pride, which God rejects. Standing in front so all could see and hear him, the Pharisee expressed his high view of himself, especially as he compared his lifestyle and values to those of the people around him. On the other hand, the tax collector humbly stood at a distance and quietly prayed. He clearly had a low view of himself as he held his head low, beat his breast, and cried out to God for mercy.

THINK ABOUT IT

To some who were confident of their own righteousness and looked down on everybody else, Jesus told this parable, "Two men went up to the temple to pray, one a Pharisee and the other a tax collector. The Pharisee stood up and prayed about himself: 'God, I thank you that I am not like other men—robbers, evildoers, adulterers—or even like this tax collector. I fast twice a week and give a tenth of all I get.' But the tax collector stood at a distance. He would not even look up to heaven, but beat his breast and said, 'God, have mercy on me, a sinner.' I tell you that this man, rather than the other, went home justified before God. For everyone who exalts himself will be humbled, and he who humbles himself will be exalted." (Luke 18:9–14)

Jesus told this parable to teach about the dangers of self-righteous pride and the blessings of humility. It applies to us today just as much as it did on the day Jesus first told the story. We need to ask ourselves which individual we are more like, the Pharisee or the tax collector.

I find that I have much in common with the Pharisee, especially when I consider my thoughts in times of public prayer, how I compare myself to people around me, and the attitude of my heart. I have been in youth-group meetings and other church meetings and have tried to impress others with my public prayers. I have read newspapers and watched the evening news and considered myself morally superior to other people in the world. I tend to think highly of myself and want others to think highly of me, too.

Like the Pharisee, church kids can tend to be self-righteous. We look at the behaviors of people in the world around us and echo the Pharisee saying to God, "Thank you that I am not like them." Then we list the good things that we have recently done: "I read my Bible almost every morning; I faithfully attend church and youth-group meetings; I do my chores around the house; I tithe; and I _____." You fill in the blank. I believe that we have all been there at some time or another. The fact that we even recount for God our "godly" behaviors reveals our hearts.

There is no doubt that we can do all the things listed above with a right heart for God, but often we take too much credit for our own spiritual health. We fail to recognize that, were it not for God's transforming grace in our lives, we would be living exactly the same as the world does. It's easy to congratulate ourselves for having the faith we do, instead of being thankful for godly influences that have helped shape us, such as family members, teachers, or church leaders. What should humble us can become our stumbling block.

Pride isn't limited to self-righteousness. Our pride can also be self-preoccupation: being overly concerned with what others think of us and strongly desiring that others would think highly of us. Shyness can result from proudly fearing saying something stupid. Thinking extensively of how we look or act in public can come from a deep desire to impress others. Regularly redirecting conversation to ourselves can be prideful self-centeredness. The bottom line is that when we are proud, we think a lot about ourselves.

A Common Battle

The battle in our hearts between pride and humility isn't new or unique. It is common to man (1 Cor. 10:13). Pride is thinking more highly of ourselves than we ought to. It says, "I am talented, gifted, morally good, and worthy of honor and praise." Humility is having an accurate, low view of ourselves and seeing ourselves as God sees us. It says, "I am a created being; I am weak and need God and others; I am naturally sinful; and God has given me talents for which he is worthy of praise."

It isn't natural to be humble. Since the fall of man, humans crave to be respected, valued, and esteemed by others. We deeply desire the praise of our parents, coaches, teachers, friends, and bosses. We want others to think we are wise and to seek us out for advice. We like it when others think we have a unique talent and are irreplaceable. Ultimately we want others to have the same high view that we have of ourselves.

We can even be prideful when it comes to our relationship with God. Viewing ourselves as morally superior to the people around us, we tend to think that God got something good when he got us. We can also wrongfully believe that we contributed to our own salvation or think that our spiritual progress depends primarily on us and not the work of the Holy Spirit within us.

> **THINK ABOUT IT**
> The promises of God toward the truly humble are almost breathtaking. The infinitely high and lofty One who lives forever promises to dwell with them, to esteem them, to give them grace, to lift them up, and to exalt them.... Humility opens the way to all other godly character traits. It is the soil in which the other traits of the fruit of the Spirit grow. [2]—JERRY BRIDGES

We can tend to be prideful, especially self-righteous. We desperately need God's help to develop a humble heart. Thankfully, the Bible has a lot to say about humility.

Take His Word for It

Let's consider a few of these promises:

1. God promises to respect and highly regard the humble.

This is the one I esteem: he who is humble and contrite in spirit, and trembles at my word. (Isa. 66:2)

2. God promises to be with and revive the humble.

For this is what the high and lofty One says—he who lives forever, whose name is holy: "I live in a high and holy place, but also with him who is contrite and lowly in spirit, to revive the spirit of the lowly and to revive the heart of the contrite." (Isa. 57:15)

3. God promises to exalt and give grace to the humble.

Whoever exalts himself will be humbled, and whoever humbles himself will be exalted. (Matt. 23:12)

"God opposes the proud but gives grace to the humble." Humble yourselves, therefore, under God's mighty hand, that he may lift you up in due time. (1 Peter 5:5–6)

4. God promises to guide the humble in what is right.

He guides the humble in what is right and teaches them his way. (Ps. 25:9)

These promises are truly amazing, especially when we remember that God—the High and Holy One, the All-Knowing, the Creator—is the one who made these promises to us. We can have complete confidence that they are true. God cannot lie, his Word is true, and his promises are guaranteed. This should give us great faith for the future and the resolve to wholeheartedly pursue humility and flee from pride.

Jesus' Teaching

Like so many of us, the disciples in Luke 9:46–48 thought highly of themselves and wanted a place of honor, but they didn't realize that becoming great required humility, lowering themselves, and serving others. Jesus made that principle clear. If anyone wants to be great, he or she must be humble in heart and action.

The Bible's standards for greatness are sharply different from the world's. The world exalts athletes, movie stars, musicians, corporate CEOs, political leaders, and the wealthy. But the promises of God in Scripture and the direct words of Jesus place value on a humble heart.

We need to make sure that our standards line up with the Word of God. We must understand that true greatness is a matter of the heart. Ultimately, it requires a humble heart.

A Look in the Mirror

> **THINK ABOUT IT**
> An argument started among the disciples as to which of them would be the greatest. Jesus, knowing their thoughts, took a little child and had him stand beside him. Then he said to them, "Whoever welcomes this little child in my name welcomes me; and whoever welcomes me welcomes the one who sent me. For he who is least among you all—he is the greatest." (Luke 9:46–48)
>
> Whoever wants to become great among you must be your servant, and whoever wants to be first must be slave of all. (Mark 10:43–44)

Let's look carefully at our lives. Where are we proud? How are we humble? Our goal is to see pride so we can fight it and recognize humility so we can grow all the more.

First, let's consider pride.

CHARACTERISTICS OF THE PROUD

Mark each one that applies to you.

____ I often talk about myself and my accomplishments.

____ When I am in a group setting, I regularly compare myself to others.

____ When I pray in public, I am quite concerned with what others think.

____ In times of public worship, I often wonder what others think of me.

____ After a youth meeting or a gathering of friends, I spend a lot of time thinking about what I said, and I wonder what people think of me.

___ In a group setting, I am hesitant to speak because I fear making a mistake or saying something stupid.

___ I look for ways to serve in public so I can be noticed and praised.

___ I do not confess sin to others because I don't want them to know my weaknesses.

___ I am driven to get straight A's in school, and nothing else will do.

___ I like it when others ask me for advice.

___ I like being the leader because people look up to me.

___ I fear leading because I may mess up in front of others.

___ I am extremely concerned with my clothes. I spend a lot of time thinking about what I will wear before going to school or out with friends.

___ I like to dress in a way that draws attention to myself.

___ I laugh at others' mistakes, but blush at my own.

Second, let's consider humility.

CHARACTERISTICS OF THE HUMBLE

Mark each one that applies to you.

___ I am amazed that the infinite, holy, all-powerful God loves me and wants to have a relationship with me.

___ I often think about how much greater God is than I am.

___ I understand my weaknesses, and I am willing to talk about them with others.

___ When I serve others, my primary goals are to bless them and honor God.

___ I enjoy leading so I can serve others as I use my gifts.

___ I enjoy following so I can assist the leader and serve others.

___ I do not mind serving in private ways, even if I am never recognized or thanked.

___ I often ask others for advice.

___ I regularly study the Bible for guidance and direction.

___ I compare my life to the standards of God.

87

____ I regularly confess my sin to others.

____ I look for ways to spend time with individuals who may not be considered cool or popular.

____ I realize I am going to make mistakes and say stupid things, so when it happens I am usually not surprised or embarrassed.

____ I know how to laugh at myself.

____ I dress modestly.

____ I realize that my gifts and talents are from God and that he deserves the glory for my accomplishments.

____ I regularly ask my parents for their advice.

____ I seriously consider my parents' advice and requests.

Did these lists help you to see your heart more clearly? Did you learn anything new about yourself? Don't be discouraged if you have a lot of checks in the first list. And don't automatically assume that you are hypocritical if you have a good number of checks in both lists. The key to this exercise is to learn more about yourself.

We need to first identify pride in our lives so we can battle it. Then we should look for ways in which we can grow in humility. Remember, the goal is to focus on our hearts, not just our behavior. When we seek to change the attitude of our hearts, our actions will change, too.

Growing in Humility

Growing in humility is a joint effort. The Holy Spirit works in our hearts as we carefully and deliberately do our part. God transforms

> ### THINK ABOUT IT
> Do we grow in humility because of God's work in our hearts or because of our efforts and our actions? Consider the following quote:
>
> Humility is a fruit of the Spirit, the result of His ministry in our hearts. But this ministry does not occur without deliberate, conscious effort on our part. The Spirit does not make us humble; He enables us to humble ourselves in these difficult situations.[3]—JERRY BRIDGES

our hearts—replacing pride with humility—through the supernatural work of the Holy Spirit and through our human effort.

So what can we do to grow in humility? Here are ten tips to consider:

1. Pray for more humility. From the start, we need to acknowledge that we need God's help. When we admit that we cannot change ourselves and that we need the help of the Holy Spirit, we humbly position ourselves at the feet of God. We need help to see ourselves accurately, to choose to be humble, to be changed as we read the Bible passages on humility, and to want to serve others. Prayer is a humble act of declaring our dependence on God.

2. Understand the immense difference between God and us. When we correctly understand who God is and how much greater he is than we are, we will be humbled.

> **THINK ABOUT IT**
> The difference between God's being and ours is more than the difference between the sun and a candle, more than the difference between the ocean and a raindrop, more than the difference between the artic snow caps and a snowflake, more than the difference between the universe and the room we are sitting in.[6]—WAYNE GRUDEM

In March 2005 *Forbes* magazine cited Bill Gates, the founder of Microsoft, as the richest man in the world with a net worth of over forty-six billion dollars.[5] That is forty-six with nine zeros after it! This is enough money to buy all thirty-two National Football League teams, all twenty-nine National Basketball Association teams, all thirty Major League Baseball teams, and all thirty National Hockey League teams, with over four billion dollars to spare. The difference in net worth between Bill Gates and us is huge, but it still doesn't even compare to the difference between God and us.

God has always existed and will always exist, and we live about eighty years. God is perfectly holy, and we are naturally sinful. God is all-powerful, and we struggle to lift a hundred pounds. God is all-knowing, and we have to be taught almost everything—even how to read, write, add, and subtract. God is wise, and we need to ask others for advice. God is everywhere at all times, and we can be in only one place at a time. Ultimately, when we know how great God is and how much greater he is than we are, we will be more inclined to be humble.

3. Be aware of your weaknesses and limitations. When we understand our weaknesses and limitations, we will be humble. We cannot sustain ourselves; we need food, water, and sleep to survive. Our parents provide food, shelter, clothing, and transportation for us. Parents and teachers instruct us in the basics of life, such as driving, manners, laundry, cooking, and academic studies. Pastors teach us about the Word of God and how it applies to our lives. Friends and family provide the companionship we crave. Modern technology—cars, microwaves, computers, video games, and MP3 players—provide things for us that we could never easily gain on our own. Most importantly, our merciful God, through the life and death of his Son, saves us when we cannot save ourselves.

We have many limitations, but understanding and admitting them will help us to have an accurate, humble view of ourselves.

4. Study God's promises to the humble. The Word of God is powerful. The author of Hebrews says that "the word of God is living and active. Sharper than any double-edged sword, it penetrates even to dividing soul and spirit, joints and marrow; it judges the thoughts and attitudes of the heart" (Heb. 4:12). When we study the Bible, God transforms our minds and hearts. When we read and think about the promises of God toward the humble, we will be motivated to pursue humility. As we learn of God's opposition to the proud, we will be determined to resist pride.

Take time to look up, think about, and pray through the following verses:

- Proverbs 8:13. God hates pride and arrogance.
- Proverbs 11:2. Pride leads to disgrace, and humility leads to wisdom.

- Proverbs 18:12. Pride leads to downfall, and humility leads to honor.
- Proverbs 22:4. Humility and fear of God lead to wealth, honor, and life.
- Isaiah 57:15. God dwells with and revives the humble.
- Isaiah 66:2. God esteems the humble.
- Matthew 5:3. The poor in spirit will receive the kingdom of heaven.
- 1 Peter 5:5–6. God opposes the proud but gives grace to and lifts up the humble.
- Other verses: Luke 18:14; James 4:6–10; Proverbs 15:33; Proverbs 16:18.

5. Study creation. Go outside on a clear evening, lie down on a blanket, and look up at the stars. They are too numerous to count. Our galaxy contains more than 100 billion stars, and there are more than 100 billion galaxies in the universe.[6] When we consider our lives in perspective of stars and galaxies, we will be humbled. And the more we study the vast universe we live in, the smaller we will feel.

If we study virtually any other part of creation, we will be humbled as well. Learning about the depths of the oceans, the reptiles of the Amazon forest, the wilds of Africa, the human body, the polar ice caps, the Rocky Mountains, and other beautiful aspects of the earth should humble us. We will realize how much we do not know, how small we are in this vast world, and how great God is in creating all of these things.

> **THINK ABOUT IT**
> When I consider your heavens, the work of your fingers, the moon and the stars, which you have set in place, what is man that you are mindful of him, the son of man that you care for him? (Ps. 8:3–4)

6. Spend time with people who are more gifted than you are. It is easy to develop an elevated view of our abilities, whether academic, athletic, artistic, or musical. We may even be one of the best among our circle of friends or at our school. But it is helpful for us to realize that many individuals are more gifted than we are.

Look for ways to spend time with people who are extremely talented. If you are a good musician, spending time with great musicians will keep you humble. If you are good at basketball, playing against high-quality basketball players will force you to be humble. If you enjoy acting, practicing and performing with talented actors and actresses will help keep you humble. When we spend time with highly talented individuals, we realize how much we have to learn and gain a realistic perspective of ourselves.

7. Learn a new skill. Learning a new skill can quickly humble us. We may be able to wield a baseball bat, but not know what to do with a skill saw. We may be able to play the piano, but not know the first thing about performing in a play.

Take a class, sign up for lessons, or read about and learn a new skill, such as carpentry, auto mechanics, sewing, or cooking. Take up a musical instrument, such as the guitar, piano, clarinet, or drums. Learn to play a new sport, such as golf, tennis, racquetball, or volleyball. When we start at the beginning, we know our limitations and our ignorance. As we learn, we are bound to make mistakes, we can grow in humility, and we should also have some fun.

8. Spend time with humble people. Our friends greatly influence us. If you want to become wise, spend time with the wise (Prov. 13:20), and if you want to grow in humility, spend time with the humble. But this isn't just about letting others' godliness accidentally rub off on you. Be intentional. Listen to humble people as they talk. Watch them as they serve. Ask them questions to learn how to be humble.

Take a minute right now to think of one or two people whom you consider humble. What is it about their lives that makes you think they are humble? Think of ways you can spend more time with them, and consider specific questions you can ask to learn more about what it means to be humble.

9. Spend time with people who are honest with you about your-self. Look for ways to spend time with people who keep you humble. We all need people who love us and speak the truth to us. We need people who will laugh at our mistakes and tease us about our imperfections. I'm not talking about cruel individuals who want to belittle us. I'm referring to good friends with whom we laugh. We joke with them, and they joke with us. Do you have any friends like this? Everyone should!

10. Serve others. Serving provides a great opportunity for us to focus on others instead of ourselves. As long as our motivation is to help others instead of to receive recognition and praise, serving can be a great way to grow in humility.

How can you help the elderly, poor, or homeless in your area? Look for ways to serve your community by picking up trash along a road, cleaning up a local park, or mowing lawns in your neighborhood. You can also serve at your church, especially in unseen ways: cleaning, working in the nursery, setting up chairs and tables, or running the sound system. Consider ways to serve young children by spending time with them, taking them to a park, or coaching a sports team. The more we focus on the needs of others, the less we will focus on ourselves. The more we serve others, the more we will learn what it means to be humble.

> **THINK ABOUT IT**
> Whoever wants to become great among you must be your servant, and whoever wants to be first must be slave of all. (Mark 10:43–44)

A Call to Action

The promises of God toward the humble are truly amazing. Yet learning to be humble goes against our nature. Thankfully, we can grow in humility. Empowered by the Holy Spirit, we can reject pride and embrace humility one choice at a time.

Are you determined to grow in humility? Do you understand that biblical greatness requires a humble heart?

Commit today to:

√ Study what God's Word says about pride and humility
√ Pray to God for grace to choose humility over pride
√ Actively pursue growing in humility

Questions for Reflection and Discussion

1. How does Robert Frost's poem help us understand the choice we have between the path of humility and the path of pride?

2. What is an example of a moment when you had to decide between humility and pride? What did you decide? How did you make your decision?

3. How would you define "pride"? "humility"?

4. Why is it hard to be humble?

5. How would you define "self-righteousness"? Why do church kids struggle with self-righteousness?

6. What does "self-preoccupation" mean? How can people tell if they are preoccupied with themselves? How is this related to pride?

7. What are the promises of God toward the humble? What do you think about these promises?

8. What prideful characteristics do you see in your life?

9. What is the role of the Holy Spirit in your growth in humility, and what is your own role?

10. Why should a person pray for humility?

11. Why would studying the attributes of God or creation help us grow in humility? Why would learning a new skill help us grow in humility?

12. Who is one humble person you know? How do you see humility demonstrated in his or her life?

Sing a New Song

"I Bow Down"[7]

Around You, such beauty
Your majesty could fill an endless sky
Holy are You, Lord
Transcendent, exalted
The heavens cannot contain Your presence
Holy are You, Lord
And as I behold Your glory, I'm undone

Chorus
I bow down at Your feet, I bow down at
  Your feet
I bow down at Your feet for You are my
  God
I bow down at Your feet, I bow down at
  Your feet
I bow down at Your feet for You are my
  God, my God

You saved me, the sinner
With crimson red You washed me white as
  snow
How I love You, Lord
You loved me, the mocker
With kindness You won my heart forever
How I love You, Lord
And as I behold this mercy, I'm undone

For more information on this song, go to www.growingupchristian.com.

Do not conform any longer to the pattern of this world, but be transformed by the renewing of your mind. Then you will be able to test and approve what God's will is —his good, pleasing and perfect will.

—ROMANS 12:2

Lord, help me to

- know the importance of having personal convictions.

- develop beliefs and values based on your Word.

- live according to my convictions.

- prepare today for the challenges I will face in the future.

6 MORE THAN MIMICKING MOM AND DAD

DEVELOPING PERSONAL BIBLICAL CONVICTIONS

A Man of Conviction

It was the summer of 1924, and a lifetime of dedicated training was finally about to pay off for Eric Liddell. This Scottish runner, renowned for both his incredible speed and his cheerful kindness to fellow competitors, was poised to take the gold medal in the Paris Olympics. He had every reason to believe he could win. The previous summer he'd won the 200-yard dash and the 100-yard dash in the London AAA championships. His time in the 100 had been unmatched in England in thirty-five years. He'd also won the Harvey Cup for the best performance of the meet.[1] Emboldened by his victories, Liddell spent the next year training for the ultimate test of determination and athletic prowess: the Olympics.

At last the fateful day came for the 100-meter race, Eric's top event. The finest runners in the world had gathered for the big day. Millions of captivated fans stayed glued to their radios and newspapers. The athletes lined up on the starting line, their lean, sculpted bodies taut with anxious determination. At the crack of the gun they flew into action, tearing down the track with surreal speed. Another chapter in Olympic history was written as each runner ripped across the finish line, and the finest athletes among them were recognized.

It was a glorious and exhilarating day on the track, and should have earned a place as one of Eric Liddell's most cherished memories. There was just one problem. He wasn't there.

Fans looking for Eric that Sunday morning would have had to venture through the doors of a humble Paris church where he could be found behind the pulpit, delivering the sermon. This exceptional athlete was a Christian above all else, and when he'd learned that the preliminary dashes for his top three events were on a Sunday, he'd stunned the world by announcing simply, "I'm not running." Though it must have been heartbreaking for a man who had trained with such fervency, there was no question in his mind that this was the right decision. Eric was a man of deep convictions, and he believed that this was a necessary step to honor Christ above his running.

Still, Eric wasn't finished yet. Though he couldn't compete in his top three events, he scrambled to prepare for the 200-meter and 400-meter. He took home an unexpected bronze medal in the 200. His qualifying times in the 400 were slow, and he was not expected to do well, but he showed up on the track with the firm assurance that God was in control. "I don't need explanations from God," he said once. "I simply believe him and accept whatever comes my way."[2]

Eric tackled the 400 like he was born for it. He flew down the track in a blur of flailing legs and thrashing arms, head high and proud. When he reached the finish line, he was five meters ahead of his nearest competitor. Eric had set a world record of 47.6 seconds, and brought home a gold medal.

It would have been easy for a celebrity like Eric to relax and enjoy his fame after such an incredible achievement, but his convictions wouldn't allow for that. Two years after taking the medal, Eric boarded a steam liner bound for China, to serve as a missionary in the country where his own parents had once been missionaries. There he met his wife, Florence, and the two were married in 1934. They had two girls, Patricia and Heather, and it seemed that they were settling into a happy life of service to Christ. Eric lived simply, often bicycling from village to village in spite of feuding Chinese warlords and Japanese invaders.

World affairs took an unfortunate turn in the late 1930s, as war began to brew in both Europe and Asia. In 1941 the threat from Japan was so high that Eric decided to send his pregnant wife and two girls home, for fear that they might be taken as hostages and used to force him to compromise his faith. Once again his deep convictions and passionate love for the gospel led him to make another significant choice: he would remain behind in China and continue ministering. It wasn't an easy choice, but Eric trusted he would be reunited with his family at the war's end.

Following Pearl Harbor, the United States entered the war, prompting Japan to round up American and British citizens and place them in internment camps. In 1943 Eric was interned at Weihsien, a former mission school that had been gutted of heat and plumbing. He continued serving as best he could, rising early each morning to study his Bible and pray, and teaching math and chemistry and coaching sports during the day. Though he missed his family terribly and regretted never having met his third daughter, he carried on his ministry by teaching Bible classes and bringing cheer to fellow prisoners.

On February 21, 1945, Eric unexpectedly collapsed and died. A brain tumor had been wearing down his body for quite some time, though he seldom complained and few people had known of his excruciating headaches. He served Christ and other people right up until the end.

In the race of life, Eric ran hard and finished strong. His convictions about God had led him to make one monumental decision after another, and the result was a life lived wholly to the glory of God. Eric left behind an incredible legacy, and he is still remembered today as a hero of the faith. His life is memorialized in the movie *Chariots of Fire*.

Eric Liddell's legacy should challenge us as Christians. What price are we willing to pay for our faith? How far would we go to honor God above ourselves? What do we really believe about God, and are we willing to stand up for those convictions?

> **THINK ABOUT IT**
> Our actions flow out of our values, which arise from our beliefs.[3]
> —JOSH MCDOWELL AND BOB HOSTETLER

This chapter is about our values and beliefs. We will examine what convictions are, why they are important, and how to develop personal convictions based on the Bible.

One of the privileges of being a Christian is having such a strong heritage of godly men and women who have gone before us. We can learn from Eric Liddell's example of bold faith and fierce commitment to his beliefs. We need that kind of commitment as we seek to live lives pleasing to God. We need to be determined to develop and live according to biblical convictions.

It Makes a Huge Difference

In Daniel chapter 3, we learn about Shadrach, Meshach, and Abednego, who refused to worship a 90-foot-high golden image that King Nebuchadnezzar had made. Even as they faced the prospect of death, they said to the king:

> O Nebuchadnezzar, we do not need to defend ourselves before you in this matter. If we are thrown into the blazing furnace, the God we serve is able to save us from it, and he will rescue us from your hand, O king. But even if he does not, we want you to know, O king, that we will not serve your gods or worship the image of gold you have set up. (Dan. 3:16–18)

Miraculously, God saved them and transformed the heart of the king in the process.

Their trust in the character and power of God guided them as they chose between worshiping an idol and honoring God, between life and death. We need the same confidence in our God, and we need the same resolve to live according to our convictions.

What we believe is of vital importance. Our beliefs shape our values, and our values shape our actions.

Failing to develop a biblical worldview and biblical convictions can be dangerous. The results of research done by George Barna and Josh McDowell and Bob Hostetler are stunning. They surveyed teens who regularly attended church, and they identified teens who had biblical beliefs and those who did not. Then they compared the lifestyles of the two groups.

Teens who did *not* hold biblical beliefs were:[4]

- Three times more likely to be disappointed in life
- More than three times more likely to lack purpose in life
- More than three times more likely to be angry with life
- Three times more likely to steal
- Three times more likely to physically hurt someone
- Four times more likely to use illegal drugs
- Seven times more likely to attempt suicide

Yes, these are teenagers who go to church most Sundays—church kids.

The research also carefully examined the specific beliefs and values of teens who seemed to be Christians. The results make it clear that it is one thing to simply profess a belief in Christ and another to possess biblically true beliefs.

Of the teenagers who seemed to be Christian:[5]

- 41 percent wrongly believed that the devil, or Satan, is not a living being but is a symbol of evil.
- 45 percent wrongly believed that all religious faiths teach equally valid truths.
- 52 percent wrongly believed that Muslims, Buddhists, Christians, Jews, and all other people pray to the same god, even though they use different names for that god.
- 52 percent wrongly believed that if a person is generally good, or does enough good things for others during his or her life, he or she will earn a place in heaven.
- 58 percent wrongly believed that when Jesus Christ lived on earth, he committed sins, like other people.

It matters greatly what *we* believe. It isn't enough to just attend church regularly or be around people who have biblical values. *Our* attitudes and behaviors flow from *our* beliefs and *our* values and not from the beliefs and values of those around us. Therefore, *our* hearts need to be shaped by the Word of God. We need biblical convictions.

What Is a Conviction?

Convictions can be weak or strong, and they can be right or wrong. Ultimately they drive our actions. Our convictions about movies determine what movies we will watch; our convictions about music will determine the CDs and radio stations we will listen to; and our convictions about truth will determine how we act toward and what we will say to others.

Our Tendency

Follow the Leader

As church kids, we have a tendency to live according to the standards of the authorities around us, especially our parents. Thankfully, many of the adults in our lives love and fear God, encourage us, and at times require us to do things that are right. But if we learn to live as a Christian should live without learning to think as a Christian should think, we set ourselves up for major challenges in the future.

Please know that I am not promoting the development of convictions contrary to those of your parents. I am urging you to develop your *own* convictions. In fact, when you pray, search Scripture, and think deeply about important topics, your beliefs and values will likely end up similar to your parents'. The difference is that the convictions you develop will be your own and not simply a copy of your parents' beliefs. When your con-

> **THINK ABOUT IT**
> Before we go any further, let's make sure we know what a conviction is. Jerry Bridges and Josh McDowell and Bob Hostetler provide two excellent definitions:
>
> A conviction is a determinative belief: something you believe so strongly that it affects the way you live.[6] —JERRY BRIDGES
>
> Having convictions can be defined as being so thoroughly convinced that Christ and his Word are both objectively true and relationally meaningful that you act on your beliefs regardless of the consequences.[7] —JOSH McDOWELL AND BOB HOSTETLER

victions are your own, you will be more prepared to resist the many temptations you will face in this world and to stand firm in times of trial.

Personal and Biblical

We need to develop our own convictions, and these convictions need to be based on the Word of God. If we base our convictions solely on our parents' experiences, values, or rules, or even just on our personal experiences, they will not hold up in times of temptation. A life-guiding conviction is one that we hold personally and one that is based on the Word of God.

Why isn't it enough simply to do the right thing? Why are *personal* convictions necessary? It greatly pleases God when we obey our parents and submit to their authority, but the reality is that someday we will no longer be under their direct authority. As we get older, we have more and more personal responsibility for our choices and actions, and we must prepare for the day when we will be on our own—or even have a family of our own. Just like driver's education classes prepare us for driving our own car, the teenage and college years are preparation for governing our own lives. We must learn to develop personal convictions as teens to be fully prepared to live God-honoring lives as adults.

Why are *biblical* convictions necessary? Convictions based just on what our parents believe may work for a time; convictions based on personal experiences may help with some situations; convictions based on personal opinions may at times guide us in decisions; and even convictions based on the values of the world may in a rare situation also honor God; but by far the best, the strongest, and the surest conviction that will guide us in every situation, decision, and temptation is a conviction formed by sound and thorough biblical study and teaching.

Take His Word for It

If we desire to develop biblical convictions, we need to let the Word of God shape our thinking and affect our hearts. The following passages teach us three important principles in developing biblical values and living the Christian life.

1. Love and study the Word of God. The psalmist describes an individual who wisely refuses to be influenced by the ungodly. Instead, he delights in the Word of God and regularly reads it, thinks deeply about it, and seeks to apply it to his life. Because reading the Bible is a delight, he loves to study it and memorize it. This type of living leads to a strong and passionate walk with God. Fed by the Word, he receives truth planted in his heart. God's goals are his goals; God's ways become his ways; and God's values become his values. He learns what it means to please God and lives according to biblical truths. Biblical convictions mark his life.

THINK ABOUT IT

Scripture describes the person who is steady, strong, and ready to face anything:

Blessed is the man who does not walk in the counsel of the wicked or stand in the way of sinners or sit in the seat of mockers. But his delight is in the law of the LORD, and on his law he meditates day and night. He is like a tree planted by streams of water, which yields its fruit in season and whose leaf does not wither. Whatever he does prospers. (Ps. 1:1–3)

THINK ABOUT IT

We need to pray for ourselves in the same way that Paul prayed:

And this is my prayer: that your love may abound more and more in knowledge and depth of insight, so that you may be able to discern what is best and may be pure and blameless until the day of Christ, filled with the fruit of righteousness that comes through Jesus Christ—to the glory and praise of God. (Phil. 1:9–11)

2. Pray that your love for God will increase. Paul sets an example for us when he prays for the Philippians.

Please join me in praying the following:

Lord, thank you for the love you have placed in our hearts. Please let it grow more and more as we increase in knowledge and depth of insight of your character and your ways. Help us to know you more fully and to understand your nature and your wisdom. Teach us about the depth of your love, compassion, and kindness. Please bring this about in our lives so we can determine what is best. When we are in moments of decision, trial, and temptation, remind us of your truth, your commands, and your values. Impress them on our hearts so that in those instances, we will choose what is best. We want to live pure and blameless lives before you, but we desperately need your help. Enable us to be faithful until you send your Son back to earth.

3. Put yourself in positions in which God can work in your heart and mind. Paul urges us to put ourselves in situations in which God and the work of the Holy Spirit can transform our hearts and minds. How do we do this? We can open our Bibles and read and learn. We can go to church and listen to the preaching of the Word. We can walk into the living room and ask our mom and dad to tell us about their faith. Or we can go to our Christian school and listen to biblical instruction in our classes and chapel services.

> **THINK ABOUT IT**
> Do not conform any longer to the pattern of this world, but be transformed by the renewing of your mind. Then you will be able to test and approve what God's will is—his good, pleasing and perfect will. (Rom. 12:2)

When we place ourselves in a position to hear from God and be transformed by the Holy Spirit, our minds will be renewed. As a result, we will know what God teaches and desires and be able to test and approve what his will is for us. We will develop true beliefs and form biblical values. Ultimately, we will possess convictions based on the truths of Scripture.

A Look in the Mirror

What about You?

In chapter 2 I referred to Catherine Marshall's book *Christy*, which recounts the story of Christy Huddleston, a well-known church kid who spent a grueling few years teaching in the Appalachian Mountains in her early twenties. Before that, Christy had grown up in the safe, nurturing environment of a Christian home and church. It had been easy to take her faith for granted, but as with any other young Christian, there came a point at which she had to ask the question: What did she *really* believe? Did she have convictions of her own?

That question was unexpectedly thrust upon her one day in the mountains, as she was discussing her faith with a bright local doctor named Dr. MacNeill, who cared for the Appalachian people. He had just told Christy he didn't consider himself a Christian when Christy asked, "But what if it turns out to be the most important thing there is?"

It was a good question, a question that Christy had doubtless learned to ask non-Christians after years of growing up in the church, but Dr. MacNeill unexpectedly turned the question around. "Why is it important to you, Christy?"

Christy's heart lurched at the realization that she'd been put on the spot. She fumbled for an answer, and after a few awkward moments mumbled, "Well, if—that is—"

An image sprang to mind of her mentor, Miss Alice, one of the finest Christians Christy knew. There was an answer! Dr. MacNeill knew Alice, too, and surely he would respect her example. Christy straightened confidently and said, "Miss Alice is just . . . the greatest person I've ever known. I wish you could have heard her the other day teaching a Bible class at the church. . . . She was telling about how the church has been the custodian of this precious truth for two thousand years . . ."

The doctor rose to his feet and stretched his big frame. "Christy," he said gently, "I did not ask you what Alice Henderson believes or for a résumé of her latest talk to her Bible class. I wanted to know why Christianity is important to *you*, what *you* believe. . . . What's your working philosophy of life?"[8]

A long, terrible silence followed. Christy wanted to answer, but her throat had constricted. Nothing came to her except stinging tears, at the painful realization that she did not know the answer to his question. His gentle rebuke hit her harder than he could have known.

That moment launched a time of deep soul-searching for Christy, as she understood for the first time that her beliefs and values were

MORE THAN MIMICKING MOM AND DAD

more a copy of Alice Henderson's than her own. She had gone from Christian parents to a Christian mentor, but had yet to adopt that faith personally. In the days and months that followed, Christy sought to find her own answers and her own convictions.

God also used other circumstances in Christy's life to force her to establish her core values. After the severe sicknesses and deaths of many people she had come to love, she was in agony as she tried to make sense of her world. It was after poring over the Word of God, particularly the book of Job, morning after morning on a quiet hillside when God broke through and met her. She ended her account by saying, "The world around me was still full of riddles for which my little mind had not been given answers. . . . But the fundamental doubt was for me silenced. I knew now: God *is*. I had found my center, my point of reference. Everything else I needed to know would follow."[9]

Can you relate to Christy's story? If an unbeliever asked you about your working philosophy of life, would you have an answer? Are your convictions your own, or does your faith rest on the experience of someone else? What beliefs and values drive your behaviors?

Let's start by considering our thoughts when we make important choices. Our thinking in moments of decision reveals a great deal about our values. What goes through our minds as we determine which radio station we will listen to in the car? What do we think about as we put on our clothes to go to school or a youth meeting? We have to gauge our thoughts in these moments of decision so we can evaluate the state of our convictions.

What questions go through your mind as you try to decide whether you should attend a movie with your friends? *Rate yourself on a scale of 1 to 10. 1 means never and 10 means always.*

____ 1. What would my parents think?

____ 2. Will anyone find out?

____ 3. Will I get in trouble?

____ 4. What do I want?

____ 5. What do my friends want me to do?

_____ 6. What would Jesus do?

_____ 7. What does the Bible say about this?

_____ 8. What does God think about this?

What influences most drive your actions? Multiple forces are at work tugging us in opposite directions, but ultimately we act. Evaluating our thoughts in moments of decision is the first step in truly assessing our convictions.

How can you tell whether you have personal convictions? Take a few minutes to consider the following questions and write your answers in a brief sentence or two. Be real. If you don't have an answer, write "I don't know." Think, be honest, and speak from your heart. What do you believe, and why do you believe it?

SELF-TEST

1. What would you say to someone who asked why you believe God exists?

2. What would you say to someone who asked why you believe the Bible is true?

3. What would you say to someone who asked how to tell whether something is right or wrong or whether something is true or false?

4. What would you say to someone who asked why it is wrong to lie?

5. What would you say to someone who asked how you know heaven is real?

6. What would you say to someone who asked you how you know Satan is real?

7. What would you say to someone who asked why you believe Christianity is true and other faiths (such as the Mormon, Jehovah's Witness, and Islamic faiths) are false?

8. What would you say to someone who asked why you attend church every Sunday?

9. What would you say to someone who asked how you know Jesus truly was God and wasn't just a great prophet?

10. What would you say to someone who asked why you are a Christian?

These are tough, important questions. What do your answers reveal about you? Do they demonstrate that you have personal beliefs, personal values, and personal convictions? Are they really yours or just copies of others'?

The next step is to determine whether our convictions are biblical. The best way to rate our convictions is to look at the motives behind our actions in light of the standards and commands of God.

SELF-TEST

How would you rate your motives in comparison to the Word of God? Rate yourself on a scale of 1 to 10. *1 means that your conviction does not line up with the Bible, and 10 means that it completely lines up with the Bible.*

____ 1. Why you attend youth-group meetings

____ 2. Why you attend church on Sundays

____ 3. Why you pray

____ 4. Why you read the Bible

____ 5. Why you have the friends you do

____ 6. Why you surf the Internet

____ 7. Why you read books

____ 8. Why you watch TV

____ 9. Why you read magazines

____10. Why you do or do not date

____11. Your goals in life

____12. Your view of Jesus

____13. Your view of the Holy Spirit

____14. How you treat your siblings

____15. How you honor your parents

Note: Consider having your parents also rate you in these fifteen areas.

What do your answers say about your motives? Do your reasons for living the way you do show a value system based on the standards of the Bible? Do you have biblical convictions?

True Convictions

Where do we go from here? What do we do if, after examining our lives, we realize that our convictions fall short of God's standards? Please know that we are not without hope. God is faithful and will help us grow. Enabled by the Holy Spirit and guided by holy Scripture, we can form God-honoring convictions. But it does take time, energy, perseverance, and faith.

Here are four tips for developing personal, biblical convictions:

1. Study the lives of godly adults around you. One of the greatest blessings of growing up in a Christian environment is that we are surrounded with wise and mature Christians we can learn from. We can have long conversations with our parents and learn about their beliefs, successes, and failures. We can watch and listen to our pastors and be inspired by their commitment to study the Word of God and apply it to their lives. We can observe our teachers and learn how they apply their Christianity to studies and to living in this secular culture. We have a great opportunity to humble ourselves and learn from the mature individuals all around us.

We need to learn to listen to them. When they talk about the message of a movie, we can see how they compare it to the Word of God. When they speak about Mormons' coming to the door, we can learn about the difference between our faith and other faiths. When they recall key events in their past, we can listen to what they learned about the character and faithfulness of God. As they explain the struggles in their hearts when they make important decisions, we can observe how they run to God in prayer and seek counsel from the Word of God and others. If we listen carefully, we can learn a lot.

We also need to ask effective questions. The external facts are rarely enough to know a person's convictions. Seek to gently probe for the thoughts and motivations behind an action or a decision. The key is asking about the "why" behind the event. Ask questions like: Why won't you watch that TV show? Why won't you mow your lawn on Sundays? Why do you go to your pastor for counsel? How did the Word of God drive your thinking when you chose your career? If we really want to learn about the values of the adults around us, we need to ask deeper questions.

2. Go to the Word of God. Remember, our tendency is to mimic the standards of our parents, pastors, and teachers, but we should strive to hold these values ourselves. That means going further than just talking with the godly adults around us. The next step is to go to the Word of God.

In 2 Timothy 3:16–17, Paul reminded Timothy, "All Scripture is God-breathed and is useful for teaching, rebuking, correcting and training in righteousness, so that the man of God may be thoroughly equipped for every good work." God has given us an amazing tool in his holy Word. It is the sword of the Spirit (Eph. 6:17) that will enable us to form convictions and live according to them.

First, we need to find out whether the Bible speaks directly to the issue we are wrestling with. Thankfully, it does teach us a lot about many topics, such as truth, marriage, divorce, Jesus, the Holy Spirit, and Satan, to name just a few. We need to study our Bibles to learn what God has to say to us.

Second, we need to understand that the Word of God speaks indirectly to many issues. The Bible is a guide God has given us to help us live the Christian life. He has provided many general principles that can help us distinguish right from wrong. Its teachings on purity help us as we surf the Internet or attend a party. The Bible's teachings about diligence and laziness guide us in how we approach schoolwork or our job. Scripture's teachings regarding loving God with all our heart, soul, and mind (Matt. 22:37) help us as we consider which career we should pursue.

The Bible is the standard of all truth. God uses it to guide us directly and indirectly in his will for our lives.

3. *Apply the truth of the Word.* When we have read and studied Scripture, we need to apply it to our daily lives. James uses the image of a mirror to explain an important truth. What do we do when we see ourselves in the mirror first thing in the morning? After the initial shock of seeing our messy hair, bad complexion, and drool-stained face, do we turn and walk away, simply forgetting or ignoring what we look like? Not a chance! We evaluate and make the appropriate adjustments. The same must be true when we look at ourselves in the mirror of the Word of God. We must evaluate ourselves—our convictions and our actions—according to Scripture, and we must apply the Word of God by making the appropriate adjustments. Are you a doer of the Word?

In Matthew 7:21, Jesus makes the sober statement, "Not everyone who says to me, 'Lord, Lord,' will enter the kingdom of heaven, but only he who does the will of my Father who is in heaven." We can look in the mirror for hours, and we can try to convince ourselves that we are fine. But unless we do something to adjust our appearance, all else is useless. The same is true regarding the Word of God and our convictions. To develop true, personal, biblical convictions, we must apply truths of Scripture to our lives. We must read it, study it, meditate on it, and evaluate our convictions according to it. And then we must put into practice the principles it teaches. Otherwise, all is lost.

> ### THINK ABOUT IT
> Do not merely listen to the word, and so deceive yourselves. Do what it says. Anyone who listens to the word but does not do what it says is like a man who looks at his face in a mirror and, after looking at himself, goes away and immediately forgets what he looks like. But the man who looks intently into the perfect law that gives freedom, and continues to do this, not forgetting what he has heard, but doing it—he will be blessed in what he does. (James 1:22–25)

4. *Pray.* All along the way as we talk with mature Christians, search Scripture, and seek to make application to our daily lives, we need to pray to God for help. God calls us to be faithful in doing our part, but he is the one who enables us and works in our hearts.

We need to pray with faith, knowing that God is loving, wise, and all-knowing. He loves us and wants the best for us. He has the best goals and knows the best ways to accomplish those goals. He knows all about our lives, the world around us, and the commandments he has given us. We can pray in faith, having confidence "that he who began a good work in [us] will carry it on to completion" (Phil. 1:6).

We need to pray for help from the Holy Spirit. God has given the Holy Spirit as a helper and a guide (John 16:13) as we try to live holy lives. Be encouraged that the same Spirit that raised Christ from the dead dwells in the heart of a believer (Rom. 8:11). The Spirit is there to help us understand God (1 Cor. 2:12–14), know God better (Eph. 1:17), and discern right from wrong (1 Cor. 2:1–16; 1 John 4:1–4). We must pray for daily help from the Holy Spirit.

Praying humbly declares our need for God. Whenever we open our Bibles, we need his help to learn his commands. We depend on him to apply his truths to our lives. We cannot change our hearts, but he can.

A Call to Action

Those of us who have grown up in Christian homes often mimic the actions or standards of our parents, and we tend to not form our own convictions. Each of us must examine the basis of our convictions. Are they personal convictions? Are they biblical convictions? We need to learn from the godly adults around us, study our Bibles, apply the Word of God to our lives, and pray to God for wisdom and discernment. Then we will be better equipped when we encounter trials and temptations. We will be more prepared to fight the good fight and walk out the Christian life.

Commit today to:

√ Evaluate your current beliefs and values
√ Form personal and biblical convictions
√ Delight in the Word of God
√ Depend on God for help as you seek to apply the truths of Scripture to your life

Questions for Reflection and Discussion

1. What are convictions? Why are they important?

2. What is a personal conviction? What is a biblical conviction?

3. What can we learn from the data presented on page 97?

4. Why do church kids tend to mimic the convictions of their parents? Why is this dangerous?

5. Can you think of any area in which you mimic your parents' convictions?

6. In the section called "A Look in the Mirror," you evaluated yourself in three different areas:

   a. What thoughts most commonly go through your mind when making a decision?

   b. What is an example of an area in which you do not have a *personal* conviction?

   c. What is an example of an area in which you do not have a *biblical* conviction?

7. Can you recall a time when you had an in-depth conversation with a mature Christian that helped you understand his or her values and convictions? What did you talk about, and what did you learn?

8. How can you use the Bible to develop a conviction about a particular topic (like going to parties, attending movies, listening to music, playing computer games, or surfing the Internet)?

9. Why is prayer vital in developing convictions?

Sing a New Song

"For Your Glory Alone" [10]

For every heart Your cross redeemed
For every triumph over sin
For every time You gave us strength
For every time Your love broke in
For every time You spared us
And delivered us from death
For every escape from Satan's snares

Chorus
Let Your victories be recounted
Let Your mighty deeds be sung
Let Your greatness be exalted for your glory
        alone
Let Your victories be recounted
Let Your mighty deeds be sung
Let Your greatness be exalted for your glory
        alone
For Your glory alone

For every slave Your power has freed
For every sickness You have healed
For every taste of heaven's joy
And for Your wondrous love revealed
For grace that's working in us
And bringing forth good fruit
For forming in us Your glorious Son

For more information on this song, go to www.growingupchristian.com.

*So then, just as you received Christ Jesus
as Lord, continue to live in him, rooted
and built up in him, strengthened
in the faith as you were taught,
and overflowing with thankfulness.*

—Colossians 2:6–7

Lord, help me to

- see all that you have done for me and given to me.

- understand the gift of salvation.

- appreciate my parents.

- be grateful for the Bible.

- love my church.

7 FAMILIAR YET THANKFUL

GROWING IN GRATEFULNESS FOR BLESSINGS FROM GOD

A Second Chance at Life

Imagine for a moment that for as long as you can remember, you have suffered from violent, uncontrollable tics. Your body quivers, jerks, and spasms from the time you wake until sleep mercifully takes you at the end of an exhausting and embarrassing day. Reading even short assignments for school can take hours because every two seconds your eyes jerk elsewhere on the page and you lose your place. Speaking a simple sentence takes intense effort and concentration. The words come out in a stuttering, jerky way, punctuated by groans and accompanied by flailing limbs. You can't play basketball. You can't pick up a glass without shattering it. The tics have such a stronghold on your body, you often can't even watch TV.

Welcome to the life of Jeff Matovic.

From the time he was three, Jeff had suffered from symptoms of Tourette syndrome, a disorder causing uncontrollable tics in some

100,000 Americans.[1] The strength of his tics made even the most mundane tasks difficult, and their visibility to the public made him the butt of jokes and laughter from others. Jeff's greatest wish in life—incomprehensible to almost all of us—was to simply sit still for a while.

Jeff tried every kind of medication available. Many of them helped for a while, but it usually wasn't long before his body adapted and he came full circle back to where he had started. He met his future wife, Debra, during a season when the medication was working well. For a while it seemed like things might turn out okay, but after they were married Jeff's medication stopped working. For a year, Debra watched Jeff's life spiral out of control. His tics grew worse than they ever had before, to the point he could no longer even function.

With his marriage on the rocks and his hope for a normal life almost gone, Jeff learned about one final option that might help him: an experimental procedure called Deep Brain Stimulation, or DBS, in which doctors implanted electrodes into the patient's brain and connected them to a kind of pacemaker. It had never been done on a Tourette patient before, so doctors weren't sure if they could help him, but Jeff was willing to try anything.

Miraculously, the procedure worked, utterly transforming Jeff Matovic's life. "We were all just crying—everyone's mouth dropped—Dr. Maddox's mouth just hit the floor," Jeff said. "Nobody expected this result, especially this quickly."[2] Today Jeff is leading a normal life, spreading hope to other Tourette sufferers that a cure might be possible. He and Debra are anticipating their first child together. All the activities he couldn't do before—reading a book, working, playing sports, even just sitting still—are now regular parts of his life.

Each of those activities is a regular, mundane part of our lives. I can't remember the last time I counted my blessings for having the physical capacity to pick up a drinking glass without breaking it, or savored the pleasure of simply sitting still. Jeff Matovic, however, takes nothing for granted. He knows what it is like to not have those simple pleasures, so every tic-free day that unfolds for him is cause for celebration and gratitude. I suspect that Jeff savors life in a way barely fathomable to most of us.

Why is that? Because for us, the tasks that make up our daily lives are a matter of routine, and after a while we cease to be grateful for the familiar. That's human nature. When we hear a story like Jeff's, we might pause and reflect on how grateful we are for the blessings in our lives, but for the most part we still take these things for granted. That leads us to the next challenge church kids must master: cultivating a grateful heart, when it's so easy to take our blessings for granted.

Our Tendency

As church kids, we can become so familiar with our Christian environment that we fail to be grateful for the many blessings we have. We have grown up hearing about God and being taught about his character and ways, but we rarely express our gratitude to God for who he is and all that he has done for us. We have Bibles all around us—three or four of our own and maybe ten in our house—but we can forget that each Bible contains the precious words of God, powerful to guide us in every aspect of life. Many of us have been born into Christian families with loving and caring parents, but we can easily take our parents for granted. We have attended church most, if not all, of our lives, but we can fail to appreciate the way God uses our local church to help our family and our personal walk with God.

Why do we often lack gratefulness for God, the Bible, our parents, and our church? It's usually for the same reason we lack gratefulness for the abilities to speak, eat, and walk—we've grown familiar with them.

The more common something is, the more we tend to take it for granted. When we know life only in the context of a Christian home, we can take it for granted. When we forget the significant difference that the Word of God makes in our lives, we will take it for granted. When we fail to see the generosity of God, we will take his kindness for granted. When we overlook the many ways our parents provide for us, we will take them for granted. And when we fail to regularly remind ourselves of the impact of our pastor and church on our relationship with God, we will take them for granted.

Christians should be the most grateful people on earth, and Christians who have had the privilege of growing up in Christian homes, with an opportunity to learn about God and hear the gospel from a young age, should be some of the most grateful Christians. But too often this isn't the case.

Take His Word for It

Treasuring God

In Matthew 13:44, Jesus told the parable of the hidden treasure: "The kingdom of heaven is like treasure hidden in a field. When a man found it, he hid it again, and then in his joy went and sold all he had and bought that field." Jesus told this parable to illustrate the value of the kingdom of heaven. In commenting on this passage, D. A. Carson said, "The kingdom of heaven is worth infinitely more than the cost of discipleship, and those who know where the treasure lies joyfully abandon everything else to secure it."[3]

Notice the attitude of the man who found the treasure. In joy, he sold all his possessions so that he could buy the field. He was joyful; he was excited; he couldn't wait to buy the field. He eagerly anticipated the moment when the land would be his and he would be the owner of the treasure.

Our attitude should be the same regarding our relationship with God. We should joyfully invest our entire lives for God, being willing to give up all because he is infinitely better.

The story doesn't tell us, but I wonder what the man thought of the treasure six months or a year after he had bought the land. Had his excitement faded? Did he regret his decision to sell all that he had? Did he still value the treasure as he had at the first moment he saw it? Had he built a house and planted some crops on the land and become so busy that he'd forgotten about the treasure?

By measuring the man's initial passion and enthusiasm, I assume that the treasure was still part of his everyday thought and a motivator for his work. But at the same time, I wonder if over time his love and passion for his treasure had diminished.

120

What a shame it would be for someone to sell all for something so valued just to see his love for it diminish over time. Unfortunately, that's often all too true of us. We so badly want a shirt, a pair of sneakers, a car, or a job, but then a month or two or a year or two later, we want new and different and better ones. This tendency can also affect our attitudes toward God, the Bible, our parents, and our church.

Why does this happen? I think it is due to a lack of gratefulness. Over time, the new possessions become familiar and our gratefulness for them fades as they collect in our closets. Our initial excitement for new opportunities diminishes, and we take privileges for granted. And the amazing blessings of growing up in a Christian home become the normal facts of life that we think little about.

Do you see the kingdom of God as a priceless treasure? Are you grateful for the privileges of growing up in a Christian home?

The Giver or the Gift

Traveling to Jerusalem, Jesus passed ten lepers, who cried out to him, "Jesus, Master, have pity on us!" Jesus heard their pleas and told them to go show themselves to the priests, and without delay they left. Along the way they realized they had been healed, and one immediately returned, threw himself at Jesus' feet, and passionately praised him. Jesus then asked, "Were not all ten cleansed? Where are the other nine? Was no one found to return and give praise to God except this foreigner?" (Luke 17:11–19).

This story provides two contrasting responses to a miraculous healing. One leper responded in thanks to Jesus, but nine did not. I imagine the nine were grateful, too, but were they more grateful for the healing or the Healer—the gift or the Giver?

We should strive to be like the one. He was incredibly excited about being healed from leprosy, but he was even more grateful for Jesus, who had healed him. He knew he would no longer be a social outcast who had to live outside the city with other lepers, but he understood that it was possible only because of Jesus' kindness to him. He knew that he was getting a second chance at life, but he was most grateful to the One who had given him the chance.

Whom are you most like—the nine or the one? Are you more grateful for the blessings in your life or the One who has given you each blessing? Are you more grateful for the gifts or the Giver?

Paul

The apostle Paul is an excellent example of someone who was consistently grateful. Look carefully at how he expresses his thankfulness:

> I thank my God every time I remember you. In all my prayers for all of you, I always pray with joy because of your partnership in the gospel from the first day until now. (Phil. 1:3–5)

> We always thank God, the Father of our Lord Jesus Christ, when we pray for you, because we have heard of your faith in Christ Jesus and of the love you have for all the saints. . . . (Col. 1:3–4)

> But we ought always to thank God for you, brothers loved by the Lord, because from the beginning God chose you to be saved through the sanctifying work of the Spirit and through belief in the truth. (2 Thess. 2:13)

Paul models joy and thankfulness, and he expresses gratefulness to God for the work God has done in the lives of the Philippians, Colossians, and Thessalonians. He knows that God is the source of all the good he has seen and heard of in these churches. He is grateful for the progress that the people are making, but he is even more grateful for the God who has granted them faith and has helped them grow in their love for Christ.

When we remember that many of Paul's epistles were written from prison, we will be inspired to be grateful regardless of our own circumstances. Understanding that his letter to the Philippians was written from a Roman jail helps us put into perspective Philippians 4:11–13: "I have learned to be content whatever the circumstances. I know what it is to be in need, and I know what it is to have plenty. I have learned the secret of being content in any and every situation, whether well fed or hungry, whether living in plenty or in want. I can do everything through him who gives me strength."

Let's strive to be Christians like Paul, who regularly expressed his gratefulness to God for God's work in the lives of those around him. Let's make it our aim to be content, joyful, and thankful in all circumstances, whether we find ourselves in times of success or failure.

God Calls Us to Be Thankful

> Speak to one another with psalms, hymns and spiritual songs. Sing and make music in your heart to the Lord, always giving thanks to God the Father for everything, in the name of our Lord Jesus Christ. (Eph. 5:19–20)

> Give thanks in all circumstances, for this is God's will for you in Christ Jesus. (1 Thess. 5:18)

I find some of God's commands easier to understand than to actually practice. Intellectually, I know that God wants me to give thanks always, no matter my circumstances, but practically speaking, this is extremely difficult.

Paul was serious, and God inspired his words. Christians should strive to be thankful in all situations of life: times of blessing or trial, successes or failures. With the help of the Holy Spirit, we can strive to accomplish this.

I find Romans 8:28 helpful when I find myself in a difficult trial: "And we know that in all things God works for the good of those who love him, who have been called according to his purpose." God promises to work all things for good for Christians, even when we don't see it. When I gain this perspective on the trials I face, I am more inclined to be grateful as I persevere through them.

A Look in the Mirror

We have examined how easy it is to take familiar blessings for granted, and we have seen how the Word of God calls Christians to be grateful and thankful. Let's turn now to look carefully at ourselves.

Are our lives distinctively marked with an attitude of gratefulness to God for the many blessings he showers on us? Are we more grateful today than we were in the past?

GRATEFULNESS SELF-TEST

On a scale of 1 to 10, rate your level of gratitude for each truth below. *1 means not grateful at all, and 10 means extremely grateful.*

___ 1. God created the world.

___ 2. God loves me.

___ 3. God sent his Son to die on the cross for me.

___ 4. God saved me.

___ 5. God never changes.

___ 6. God hears all my prayers and knows each one of my needs.

___ 7. God is holy and never sins.

___ 8. God is perfectly wise and knows everything.

___ 9. God has given me the Bible to help me grow in my knowledge of him and his will.

___10. God has given me the Bible to encourage and direct me.

___11. God helps me to read the Bible daily.

___12. God has placed me in a Christian family.

___13. God gave me my parents.

___14. God uses my parents to tell me the gospel.

___15. God uses my parents to teach and train me in his ways.

___16. God has placed my family in our church.

___17. God uses my pastor to help me grow in my knowledge of God.

___18. God has provided many opportunities for me to serve in my church.

Go back to each of your answers above and rate your level of gratefulness today compared to your gratitude a year ago, using the following symbols: "+" means that your gratitude has increased, "–" means that it has decreased, and "=" means that it has stayed the same.

What do your answers tell you about your current level of gratitude? Overall, are you more or less grateful today than you were a year ago?

Developing a Grateful Lifestyle

Joni

When Joni plunged into the cool water of the Chesapeake Bay on a leisurely July afternoon, she had no idea how her life was about to change. She broke the murky water in a perfect dive, but instead of gliding through to the surface, her senses exploded with the unexpected. Her head struck something hard. She jerked out of control in the water, ears ringing, something like a shock coursing through her entire body. Next thing she knew, she was lying facedown in the grinding sand, terrified and unable to move. While the currents lifted and settled her body again, she fought ferociously to free her arms and feet, but they felt pinned in place. Her lungs began to burn. If she didn't breathe soon, she would drown. The nearness of death, coupled with the confusing and frightening inability to control her body, led to an inescapable, overwhelming sense of panic. At the last possible moment her sister dragged her out of the water, and she gasped in the salty air. Joni was alive, but would soon discover she was completely paralyzed.[4]

What would you feel in the wake of such a devastating accident? How would you view God? Would you be grateful or resentful? I know my first instinct wouldn't be to see paralysis as a blessing.

Yet today Joni travels around the country, speaking about her faith in Jesus Christ. She sees the accident as an act of divine love: God's reaching down to pull her from a life of disillusionment and complacency. She doesn't know why the accident had to happen, but she's seen good fruit come of it through her transformed life. "I really am [happy]. I wouldn't change my life for anything. I even feel privileged. God doesn't give such special attention to everyone and intervene that way in their lives. . . . I'm really thankful He did something to get my attention and change me."[5]

Joni Eareckson Tada is an inspiration to us all. She has seen God work through extreme trials, and she has learned to be grateful to God for his plan for her life. Like Joni, we need to understand how God works all things for our good. Whether we find ourselves in a time of prosperity or need—blessing or trial—we have reason to be thankful to our ever-present and ever-faithful God.

Lasting Gratitude

We need to develop a grateful heart if we hope to maintain lasting gratitude. There are no quick fixes when it comes to developing a joyful and grateful lifestyle. Gratitude is an issue of the heart and cannot be faked for very long, especially thankfulness for God, the Bible, our parents, and our church. The good news is that when we address our hearts, gratitude will overflow into virtually every aspect of our lives.

Here are seven tips for growing in gratitude:

1. Ask God for help. Just like any other area of our lives, we need God's help to change. We need to start by communicating our need to God and our dependence on him by praying. He is the one who will enable us to take the appropriate steps to change. He transforms our hearts as we faithfully do our part. We need to ask him specifically for more gratefulness for the many blessings in our lives.

2. Build a strong relationship with Christ.

So then, just as you received Christ Jesus as Lord, continue to live in him, rooted and built up in him, strengthened in the faith as you were taught, and overflowing with thankfulness. (Col. 2:6–7)

The foundation of an attitude of thankfulness is a life lived in fellowship to Christ.[6] —Jerry Bridges

Thankfulness flows out of a heart that is rooted in Christ. If Christ is the Lord of our lives, we will live in him, be built up in him, and be strengthened in him. Ultimately we will find ourselves overflowing with thankfulness to him for all that he has done on our behalf.

This means we need to develop a stronger relationship with God. We need to make the effort to sow seed that will yield fruit in our relationship with him and cause us to become more rooted and built up in him, naturally overflowing with thankfulness.[7]

3. Recount the undeserved blessings from God.

Thankfulness to God is a recognition that God in His goodness and faithfulness has provided for us and cared for us, both physically and spiritually. It is a recognition that we are totally dependent upon Him; that all that we are and have comes from God.[8] —Jerry Bridges

We are never thankful for what we think we deserve. We are deeply thankful for what we know we don't deserve.[9] —Randy Alcorn

When we understand that a personal relationship with God is a completely undeserved blessing, we will overflow with thanks to God. When we comprehend that the Bible is a generous gift to us, we will love and treasure it. When we realize that we do not deserve the parents we were given, we will be all the more grateful for them. When we grasp the sacred role that the church plays in accomplishing God's will on earth, we will understand what a unique opportunity it is to grow up in a church.

4. *Study specific passages of Scripture.* To grow in gratitude for specific things, we need to study specific sections of the Bible that focus on them.

Here are a few passages for each of the four areas that we have focused on in this chapter. Take a few moments to look each of them up.

God:

Psalm 8: "O Lord, our Lord, how majestic is your name in all the earth! You have set your glory above the heavens. . . ."

Isaiah 40:25–31: " 'To whom will you compare me? Or who is my equal?' says the Holy One. . . ."

Romans 8:31–39: ". . . Who shall separate us from the love of Christ? Shall trouble or hardship or persecution or famine or nakedness or danger or sword? . . . No, in all these things we are more than conquerors through him who loved us. For I am convinced that neither death nor life, neither angels nor demons, neither the present nor the future, nor any powers, neither height nor depth, nor anything else in all creation, will be able to separate us from the love of God that is in Christ Jesus our Lord."

The Bible:

Psalm 119: "Blessed are they whose ways are blameless, who walk according to the law of the LORD. Blessed are they who keep his statutes and seek him with all their heart. . . ."

2 Timothy 3:16: "All Scripture is God-breathed and is useful for teaching, rebuking, correcting and training in righteousness, so that the man of God may be thoroughly equipped for every good work."

Hebrews 4:12: "For the word of God is living and active. Sharper than any double-edged sword, it penetrates even to dividing soul and spirit, joints and marrow; it judges the thoughts and attitudes of the heart."

Our Parents:

Proverbs 6:20–22: "My son, keep your father's commands and do not forsake your mother's teaching. Bind them upon your heart forever; fasten them around your neck. When you walk, they will guide you; when you sleep, they will watch over you; when you awake, they will speak to you."

Ephesians 6:1–3: "Children, obey your parents in the Lord, for this is right. . . ."

Colossians 3:20: "Children, obey your parents in everything, for this pleases the Lord."

Our Church:

Romans 12:4–8: "Just as each of us has one body with many members, and these members do not all have the same function, so in Christ we who are many form one body, and each member belongs to all the others. . . ."

1 Corinthians 12:12–27: "The body is a unit, though it is made up of many parts; and though all its parts are many, they form one body. So it is with Christ. . . ."

Ephesians 4:3–16: "It was he who gave some to be apostles, some to be prophets, some to be evangelists, and some to be pastors and teachers, to prepare God's people for works of service, so that the body of Christ may be built up. . . ."

5. Regularly communicate thanks. We need to make a practice of verbalizing our appreciation to God, our parents, and our church leaders. If we give just a few moments of our time to considering ways in which God, our parents, and our church have blessed us, we will have a lot to communicate.

When we pray, we need to make it a practice to thank God for all that he has done for us: saving us, giving us his Word, remaining faithful to his promises, allowing us to grow up in a Christian home, and more. There is so much we can thank God for.

We also need to faithfully thank our parents for their love for and generosity to us. They have provided us with a home, food, and clothing. They give us wise counsel and watch out for us. They have pointed us to God and taught us about the Bible from a young age. We shouldn't let a day go by when we haven't thanked them for something.

Whether our pastor, a ministry team leader, or a faithful servant, many individuals in our churches need to hear our thanks. We should make it a practice to express our gratitude for our church leaders. They provide spiritual oversight for our families, and they invest so much of their time and energy into the people of our churches. We also need to look around for people who serve behind the scenes and make a huge difference in the life of the church. Consider thanking the cleaning staff, the sound crew, and the setup team. It will encourage them, and bless you, too.

But remember, when you thank people, be sure to first and foremost thank God for them and their hard work. God is at work in their lives and deserves the first round of our gratitude.

6. Seek to develop stronger relationships with Mom and Dad. The world says teenagers should break away from their parents and live more and more independent lives. Most people expect teens to have a poor relationship with their parents, whether they are Christian teens or not. This is a lie that we must reject. The Word of God calls children to honor and obey their parents, and the standards do not change when someone turns 13, 16, or 19.

God has established these guidelines for your good. No one loves you more than your parents do, and no one wants you to succeed more than they do. The teenage years are difficult, but instead of running *from* your parents, this is a season when you need to be running *to* them. Their wisdom coupled with their love makes them your greatest advocates. No, they won't let you do whatever you want, but they will help you do what is best. Sometimes "no" is the most loving answer you can receive.

What can you do today to help strengthen your relationship with your parents? Be countercultural: spend time with your parents, talk to them, and listen to their advice!

7. Get more involved at church. Nothing is more effective in increasing our affections and gratitude for the local church than getting more involved. When we volunteer to put up decorations for a youth banquet, we have a lot more fun when the event takes place. When we serve on the sound team, we will be grateful for all the people who work hard behind the scenes to make an event run smoothly. When we join our pastor's Bible study, we will appreciate the wisdom God has given him. When we get more involved, we will become grateful for the people at our church and for God working through its ministries and events.

How can you get more involved with your church today?

Christians should overflow with gratitude to God, and church kids should be particularly grateful for the Christian environment they have grown up in.

A Call to Action

Are you a grateful person? Is it clear to those around you? Don't fall into the trap of being so familiar with your Christian environment that you fail to be grateful for it. If you are not as grateful as you should be, ask God to help you change. With the help of the Holy Spirit and a reminder of the many blessings you have received, you will find your heart overflowing with gratitude. Then make sure you express it both to God and to others. Thank God for his Word, for his character, and for transforming your heart. Communicate your gratefulness to your parents and your church leaders.

Commit today to:

√ Be grateful first and foremost for God and his work in your life

√ Be grateful for growing up in a Christian environment

√ Love and value the Word of God

√ Regularly communicate your love and appreciation to your parents

√ Praise God for your church

Questions for Reflection and Discussion

1. Why does our gratitude for someone or something tend to fade over time? Why do we often lack gratitude for things we are familiar with?

2. Why should we be grateful for growing up in a Christian environment?

3. What is the difference between being thankful for the Giver and being thankful for the gift? How are they related?

4. Why is it so hard to be thankful in all circumstances?

5. In the section "A Look in the Mirror," what did you learn about your gratefulness for God, the Bible, your parents, and your church? Is your gratefulness increasing, decreasing, or staying the same?

6. How would you counsel a friend who wants to grow in gratitude?

7. What is the role of prayer in growing in gratitude? What is the role of the Bible in growing in gratitude?

8. Why do many teens have a poor relationship with their parents? What do you think God wants the relationship between a teenager and his or her parents to look like?

9. What things do teenagers tend to do that harm their relationship with their parents? What is one thing you can do this week that will strengthen your relationship with your parents?

10. How can you get more involved in your church? Who is one person you can thank for his or her service in your church?

Sing a New Song

"I Stand in Awe" [10]

You are beautiful beyond description
Too marvelous for words
Too wonderful for comprehension
Like nothing ever seen or heard
Who can grasp Your infinite wisdom?
Who can fathom the depth of Your love?
You are beautiful beyond description
Majesty enthroned above

Chorus
And I stand, I stand in awe of You
I stand, I stand in awe of You
Holy God to whom all praise is due
I stand in awe of You

You are beautiful beyond description
Yet God crushed You for my sin
In agony and deep affliction
Cut off that I might enter in
Who can grasp such tender compassion?
Who can fathom the mercy so free?
You are beautiful beyond description
Lamb of God who died for me

For more information on this song, go to www.growingupchristian.com.

Watch your life and doctrine closely.
—1 TIMOTHY 4:16

Lord, help me to

- love the truth.

- know the basic truths of the Christian faith.

- love you more as I seek to learn sound doctrine.

- live according to the truths you have given me in the Bible.

8 BUILDING A FIRM FOUNDATION

LOVING THE TRUTHS OF SCRIPTURE

The Most Dangerous Road in the World

The natives say it is best to travel La Cumbre to Coroico at night, and Keith was beginning to understand why. At least at night a traveler would be blissfully unaware that certain death loomed mere feet away. Keith had regrettably decided to travel in the late morning, and his stomach was churning as he peered out the window of the forty-passenger bus at the sheer rock face plummeting into the cloud-swept vista below. There were no guardrails. Keith dared to press his face against the glass for a better look, but drew back at the dizzying sense of vertigo that ensued. He couldn't even see ground between the bus and the drop-off.

Keith instinctively scooted away from the window. He tried to face straight ahead, but the view out front wasn't any more reassuring. The narrow road had literally been cut into the mountainside, snaking around blind corners and twisting back into view farther ahead. At any moment, Keith expected a semi to come barreling around a corner and smash their rickety old bus right over the edge. It was crazy enough that the Bolivians used this tiny gash in the mountain as a road. It was downright suicidal that they used it both directions at once.

Sadly, that was no exaggeration. La Cumbre to Coroico killed somebody every ten days. In the hour they'd been driving, Keith had spotted the wreckage of six cars and twelve grave markers, grisly reminders that this road, which wound between the Inca trail and the city of Coroico, was reputed to be the most dangerous in the world. With four hours left of travel, Keith wondered if there would be a marker left for him. Hands down, this was his most terrifying experience so far as a missionary in Bolivia. He closed his eyes and prayed.

Keith was halfway through the agonizing trip, trying unsuccessfully to nap as the bus jostled and creaked up a steep, winding stretch of road, when he heard the wheezing hiss of old brakes. His eyes snapped open to see that they had stopped behind another truck, evidently broken down—of all places—on the mountain side of the road. Keith's eyes widened at the sight of the narrow gap between the truck and the sheer drop-off. There was no way to get around, and turning around would be impossible out here. It looked like they were stuck.

He could scarcely believe it when, after a long moment's consideration, the driver put the bus back in gear and started creeping forward. Keith exchanged a panicked glance with another passenger. It was bad enough that the driver had to take the bus right to the edge of the cliff to squeeze through such a tiny gap, but to make things worse, a blind corner lurked just ahead. Anything that came around that corner might not have time to stop.

The driver pulled carefully up to the truck, and by some inexplicable miracle managed to squeeze alongside, so close to the cliff edge that Keith felt as if he was hanging over it. He leaned toward the center of the bus, out of an irrational fear that getting too near the edge might send them toppling over. Suddenly the guardrail seemed like humanity's grandest invention.

They were nearly clear of the truck when another bus suddenly appeared around the blind corner ahead. Fortunately, both drivers were going slowly, and braked to a stop without incident, but the timing could not have been worse. The rule of the road dictated that downhill traffic had the right-of-way. With Keith's bus blocked by the downhill bus, and pinned to the cliff edge by the disabled truck, that meant that they had only one option: backing down the treacherous slope until they found a place wide enough to pass. It had been difficult enough going forward. If they survived that, they would have to pass the truck once again.

The driver stared attentively into his side-view mirror and let the bus roll back a few inches. Keith sucked in his breath. The next several minutes passed in a blur of fear and fervent prayer.

When it was all over, Keith was trembling and exhausted from the adrenaline surge. Soon they were on their way again, the offending truck lost in a trail of dust behind them. After another two hours on the deadly road, they reached Coroico. Keith gladly fled the bus, thrilled to be on safe ground and feeling as if he'd had the adventure of a lifetime.

Guardrails

La Cumbre to Coroico may be the most dangerous road in the world for a variety of reasons: it's a dirt road, it is narrow, it is cut into the side of a mountain range, it reaches high altitudes, and there is the constant threat of mudslides. The absence of guardrails or barriers on its outer edge makes it dangerously easy for a vehicle to slide off the road and plummet the passengers to their deaths.

Installing guardrails on this remote mountain road would be extremely difficult and it wouldn't prevent all deaths, but it would certainly help. Guardrails could at least let drivers know where the road stops, and they could prevent many cars from sliding over the edge.

Christians need guardrails, too. We live in a secular world with a large range of standards and values. The messages we hear and the temptations we face—in music, movies, magazines, and more—

137

> ### THINK ABOUT IT
> But properly understood, biblical truths are guardrails that protect us from plunging off the cliff. A smart traveler doesn't curse the guardrails. He doesn't whine, "That guardrail dented my fender!" He looks over the cliff, sees demolished autos below, and is grateful for the guardrails.[1] —RANDY ALCORN

constantly bombard us with an abundance of lies, and it is often difficult to discern the truth in the midst of it all.

Thankfully, God has provided us with a guidebook to living the Christian life—the Bible.

Biblical truths provide us with a standard to measure all of life. They provide boundaries on our left and right and help us safely live out our faith. They serve as guardrails along the road of life.

Our Tendency

Doctrine

The term "doctrine" may sound like a stuffy word used only by seminary students and biblical scholars, but it really is a simple term that refers to biblical truth. The study of doctrine is the study of what the entire Bible teaches about a particular topic. For example, the doctrine of God focuses on what all of Scripture teaches about God—his character, attributes, and ways.

Because every Christian needs to know what the Bible teaches, every Christian needs to study and learn doctrine. But the goal isn't just to learn *about* doctrine; the goal is to grow in our love for God as we learn the truths of Scripture. The more we know about the Bible, the stronger our affections should be for our Lord. And the more we love him, the more we will want to live in a way that pleases him.

Church Kids and Doctrine

Having grown up in Christian homes, we have been taught the holy Scriptures from a young age. Whether in family Bible studies, Sunday school, or personal times of reading, we have learned the stories of the Bible. Having listened to hundreds of sermons at church

THINK ABOUT IT

We face a particular danger. J. C. Ryle described it as possessing secondhand knowledge of biblical truths:

But there is one class of persons . . . which in these days is in peculiar danger. . . . The persons I speak of are not thoughtless about religion: they think a good deal about it. They are not ignorant of religion: they know the outlines of it pretty well. But their great defect is that they are not "rooted and grounded" in their faith. Too often they have picked up their knowledge secondhand, from being in religious families, or from being trained in religious ways, but have never worked it out by their own inward experience. Too often they have hastily taken up a profession of religion under the pressure of circumstances, from sentimental feelings, from animal excitement, or from a vague desire to do like others around them, but without any solid work of grace in their hearts. Persons like these are in a position of immense danger.[2]
—J. C. Ryle

and youth meetings, we have heard many of the truths of the Christian faith.

Because we know more of the stories and facts of the Bible than people twice our age, we can tend to think we know enough about biblical truths. Too quickly we can become satisfied with knowing basic truths of the Bible as they are passed on to us and not think deeply about them to make sure we personally understand and believe them. We gain secondhand knowledge of the Bible and fail to make it firsthand knowledge that will rightly shape our thinking and drive our actions.

It is like the difference between someone telling us about the Grand Canyon and personally visiting it. Books and pictures may describe it in detail, but to experience and fully understand the beauty of the Grand Canyon, we need to visit it ourselves.

We need a personal relationship with God—a faith and a walk of our own. We need to personally know, believe, and apply every truth of Scripture not because our parents or pastors tell us they

139

are true, but because we personally know they are true. We need firsthand knowledge of the Word of God and firsthand love for our Savior.

What Happened to Him?

Have you ever known a church kid who seemed to totally abandon his faith after high school? Maybe he went away to college or got a job in another area, but when he had the freedom to choose whatever he wanted, he decided to walk away from the faith he grew up with. Why does this happen?

I believe it is due to a lack of a personal relationship with God and a firsthand knowledge of biblical truths. When our beliefs are just copies of our parents' values or what's expected of us at our Christian school, we probably do not have genuine faith. When we believe certain biblical truths only because our pastor says so or our teachers believe them, we have a shallow faith. And if these never change, we will surely face a challenging season someday in the future.

It is far too common to hear of church kids who have walked away from their faith. I have seen a good number of my friends and my students, who appeared to be walking with God when they were younger, abandon the truths they grew up with. This fact has been a driving force for me as I write. I pray that God uses this book to prevent individuals from experiencing the heartache of turning from God and pursuing the world.

> ### THINK ABOUT IT
> J. C. Ryle again has excellent insight for us:
>
> Children of religious parents . . . often grow up professing a religion without knowing why, or without ever having thought seriously about it. And then when the realities of grown-up life begin to press upon them, they often astound everyone by dropping all their religion, and plunging right into the world. And why? They had never thoroughly understood the sacrifices which Christianity entails. They had never been taught to "count the cost."[3]
> —J.C. RYLE

140

It isn't enough to know the facts of the Christian faith. We need to think seriously about them, know why they are important, and take them to heart. The depth of our knowledge today will affect the strength of our walk in the future.

Deep and Strong

In 1883 the Brooklyn Bridge opened, connecting the boroughs of New York and Brooklyn. Its architectural design astounded everyone with its symmetry and two giant support towers.

The bridge took thirteen years to build because many challenges and setbacks arose along the way. The main architect knew that the two tall support towers would need to go deep down into the ground below the river. To rest on bedrock, one tower had to go down almost forty-five feet and the other over a hundred feet—an extremely difficult task in that day. But it was essential that the workers dig deep enough for the towers to support the structure for years to come.

The task proved to be extremely difficult and risky. The workers had to perform their job at such a great depth that some of them died from the punishing effects of high atmospheric pressure—a condition called the bends, in which nitrogen bubbles get into the bloodstream and block vital organs from receiving oxygen. Finally the Brooklyn Bridge was completed, and since 1883 it has been a symbol of stability and excellence in architecture. The bridge still stands strong today because years ago the workers did the hard work of digging deep.[4]

We live in a world where many do not believe in absolute truth. Most people think truth varies from person to person and certainly isn't determined by the standards of the Bible. The older we get, the more we will come face to face with the message and values of the world. To effectively prepare ourselves and to ensure that we will hold strong in the future, we need to dig deeply today. We need to accurately know the truths of Scripture and understand why they are important. We must strive for firsthand knowledge of the truths of God. Then we can hold strong no matter the situation or trial we will face in the future.

We cannot make the mistake of laying a shallow foundation that is merely inches deep. We cannot simply know the stories of the Bible and attempt to repeat what we think our parents believe. We cannot be satisfied with surface knowledge. We cannot take our faith casually. We cannot afford to halfheartedly approach the Bible, what we believe, or why we believe it.

We want to avoid being like the individuals on La Cumbre to Coroico with no guardrails, living our lives without the protection that God has provided. And we cannot presume that guardrails are in place in our lives by assuming that we already have enough biblical knowledge. We need to make sure to lay a strong foundation in our spiritual lives by loving and pursuing sound biblical doctrine.

Take His Word for It

Foundations

Jesus wrapped up the Sermon on the Mount by stressing the importance of knowing and applying the truths of his teachings. He contrasted two different builders:

> **THINK ABOUT IT**
> Randy Alcorn describes the weak foundations of many Christians:
>
> Theological illiteracy and unbelief have dramatically increased among evangelical Christians in the past three decades. Churches are in desperate need of a fresh infusion of truth, a vigorous teaching of biblical doctrine. Without it, we and our children will have nothing to offer this truth-deprived world.[5]
> —RANDY ALCORN

Therefore everyone who hears these words of mine and puts them into practice is like a wise man who built his house on the rock. The rain came down, the streams rose, and the winds blew and beat against that house; yet it did not fall, because it had its foundation on the rock. But everyone who hears these words of mine and does not put them into practice is like a foolish man who built his house on sand. The rain came down, the streams rose, and the winds blew and beat against that house, and it fell with a great crash. (Matt. 7:24–27)

The fundamental difference between the two houses was the foundation. The first house had a foundation on secure rock and stood strong, but the second house had a sand foundation and crashed to the ground in the storm.

When we hear, know, and apply biblical truths, we wisely lay a strong foundation to our faith, and we will be ready and able to face the challenges of life. We need to strive to learn the truths of Scripture and put them into practice.

To stand strong in our faith and to impact our culture for Christ, we need to have a firm understanding of the truths of Scripture and apply them to our lives. We need to build on the rock.

The Great Commission

The gospel of Matthew ends with Jesus appearing to his disciples after his resurrection. He gives them (and each of us) an assignment:

> All authority in heaven and on earth has been given to me. Therefore go and make disciples of all nations, baptizing them in the name of the Father and of the Son and of the Holy Spirit, and teaching them to obey everything I have commanded you. And surely I am with you always, to the very end of the age. (Matt. 28:18–20)

This passage is often a theme verse for missionaries, but it is much more than instructions just for Christians who travel overseas. Jesus calls all of his followers to make disciples, baptizing them and teaching them to obey all that he has commanded.

Notice the teaching component of the Great Commission. Jesus expects his followers to know his commands and be prepared to teach them to others. He doesn't just want knowledgeable Christians; he wants us to be acting Christians. He wants us to obey him and teach others to obey him, too.

To effectively carry out the Great Commission, we need to study doctrine. We need to know the basic truths of the Christian faith and pass them on to others. Our goal should be to personally love our Savior and inspire others to love him, too.

Life and Doctrine

First Timothy 4:16 is a simple and important sentence. Paul, who had personally trained Timothy and set him in place as the pastor of the Ephesian church, knew the importance of watching his life and doctrine closely. Timothy needed to hear it in the first century, and we need to hear it today.

We need to watch carefully to ensure that our lives and beliefs are consistent with Scripture. We need to examine what we know and how we put it to work as we strive to follow the standards of God.

> ### THINK ABOUT IT
> Paul wrote two letters to Timothy from a Roman prison shortly before he was put to death. Paul had an amazing love for Timothy and must have had a deep desire to write and give this faithful pastor some final instructions before his death:
>
> Watch your life and doctrine closely. (1 Tim. 4:16)

Benefits

To get a driver's license, we have to pass a driver's education class. We have to learn the basic rules of the road and log hours of driving. Our focus isn't just on knowing all the rules; it's on obtaining our license and experiencing the joy and freedom of being able to drive a car on our own.

The Christian life is similar. We need to study the Bible and learn the truths of Scripture, but our main goals are to grow in our love for God and experience the joy and freedom of life in Christ. Knowing biblical truths isn't the end in itself, but it is a means toward the end.

As we study what the Bible teaches about God, Christ, man, salvation, the Word of God, and the future, we will see God place guardrails in our lives to protect us from being deceived by the world's temptations. We will experience freedom in our walk with God, and we will more effectively serve him. As we grow in our knowledge of biblical truth, we will also find ourselves growing in our love for God, trusting him more easily, wanting to worship him, eager to obey him, peaceful in trials, and more prepared to counsel and care for others.

To build a strong foundation for our faith, we need to know and apply the teachings of Scripture. If we want to fully accomplish the Great Commission, we need to seek to know sound biblical doctrine. At every turn in our lives, we need to watch our life and doctrine carefully so that we can experience the joy and freedom that are in Christ. In the end, we will experience the amazing benefits of knowing and loving our gracious Lord.

A Look in the Mirror

Now that we have discussed the importance of pursuing sound doctrine, let's look at our current knowledge of the truths of the Bible. First we'll examine why we think certain truths are important, and then we'll consider how key doctrine applies to everyday circumstances.

WHY IS IT IMPORTANT?

Below are nine truths from the Word of God. Briefly explain why each is important in the Christian faith.

Scripture says that:

1. God never changes.
2. God does not lie.
3. God works all things for good for Christians.
4. Every person is born sinful and has a sinful nature.
5. Salvation is by faith alone.
6. We reap what we sow.
7. All Scripture is God-breathed and God-inspired.
8. One day everyone will stand before the judgment seat of God.
9. Someday Jesus Christ will return.

MATCH THE TRUTH WITH THE SITUATION

Which truths listed in letters a–e will help you with situations 1–10? Match at least one letter with each situation.

___ 1. You cannot sleep at night because you are anxious about a big test tomorrow.

___ 2. You need to encourage your friend whose mother was just diagnosed with cancer.

___ 3. You're trying to decide what college to attend when you graduate.

___ 4. You need to decide whether you will attend a particular movie.

___ 5. You just had a conflict with your parents.

___ 6. Your employer called and asked you to work all day on Sunday.

___ 7. You just discovered that your best friend cheated on his history test.

___ 8. You cannot overcome a particular sin in your life.

___ 9. Your friend asks you what's so important about attending church.

___10. Your college professor says the Bible isn't inspired by God. He believes it is just good writings by good people from the first century.

    a. Truths regarding attributes of God (e.g., all-knowing, all-powerful, unchanging)

    b. Truths regarding the Word of God (e.g., inspired by God, powerful, applicable to our lives)

    c. Truths regarding the nature of man (e.g., created in God's image, sinful by nature, able to have a personal relationship with God)

    d. Truths regarding Christ and his death on the cross (e.g., Jesus lived a sinless life, his death paid the price for my sins, his righteousness is credited to me)

    e. Truths regarding the church (e.g., God wants unity in the church, God has equipped people to serve in the church, believers are to gather together)

Do you love the truths found in Scripture? Do you have firsthand knowledge of them? Do you know how to apply them to everyday life?

Growing in Knowledge

So what do we do if we want to grow in our knowledge of sound doctrine but we don't know where to start?

Here are four tips to consider:

1. Start with the right motive. We cannot pursue biblical knowledge just to grow in knowledge. Understanding doctrine isn't the goal. Loving God and living in a way that pleases him need to be our aims. Knowledge tends to puff us up (1 Cor. 8:1–2), but a genuine relationship with God with a true knowledge of his character and love will keep us humble (Isa. 6:5; Ps. 8:3–4).

2. Seek to have knowledge with passion. Have you ever known someone who is passionate about something but knows very little about it? He may be a ten-year-old who loves basketball, but doesn't know much about the details of the game. If you ask him about man-to-man defense or a full-court press, he will probably get confused and be hard to understand. His pursuit of basketball may even be a passing phase unless his knowledge of the game grows.

Christians who are passionate about God but lack a depth of knowledge of biblical truth are similar. They can be hard to follow and lack consistency in their walk. They may go through extreme ups and downs and fail to grow if they do not increase in their knowledge of the Bible.

Have you ever met someone who is knowledgeable about something but has little passion for it? This may be a classmate who is naturally gifted in math, but doesn't really enjoy it. She may find math class boring and homework a waste of time because she quickly understands the concepts. She tends to complain about math and looks down on others who do not get the concepts quickly. She certainly doesn't inspire anyone to love and pursue the study of math.

Christians can be like this, too. We can know the stories and the facts of the Bible but fail to have a passion for God and his Word. We

> **THINK ABOUT IT**
>
> If we pursue theological knowledge for its own sake, it is bound to go bad on us. It will make us proud and conceited. The very greatness of the subject matter will intoxicate us, and we shall come to think of ourselves as a cut above other Christians because of our interest in it and grasp of it.[6] —J. I. PACKER
>
> We must seek, in studying God, to be led to God.[7] —J. I. PACKER

147

can understand and even verbalize the key truths of the Christian faith, but not be excited about any of them. This type of knowledge is empty and fails to represent the loving God of the Bible, who is worthy of all obedience.

Our goal needs to be knowledge with passion. Nothing else will do. Knowledge with passion leads to a lasting and fulfilling relationship with God and inspires others to love God in the same way.

3. Focus on the doctrines of God, man, and salvation. So where should we focus our study? I suggest three basic areas: the doctrine of God, the doctrine of man, and the doctrine of salvation.

The doctrine of God refers to what the Bible teaches about God's character, attributes, and ways. God does not lie, his love never fails, he is merciful and gracious, and in love he sent his Son to die for us. God is eternal, all-knowing, all-powerful, unchanging, and holy. God controls all things, faithfully upholds his promises, and judges the living and the dead.

The doctrine of man focuses on what the Bible teaches about humans. We are created in the image of God. We are born with a sinful nature, but through Jesus Christ we can have a relationship with God. We can grow in our knowledge of God and battle the sin in our hearts.

The doctrine of salvation covers God's plan of redemption. God loves us and sent his Son to earth to redeem us. Jesus lived a sinless life and died on the cross to atone for our sins. Jesus rose from the dead and now sits at the right hand of the Father. We are saved by faith alone, but genuine faith should lead to God-honoring works. When God saves us, he regenerates our hearts and makes us new creatures. We are called to proclaim the gospel to the world.

The study of doctrine goes far beyond these three areas, but I think they are the best places to start.

4. Use helpful tools as you study. How do we study these areas? Where do we start?

The best resource I know of is the book *Bible Doctrine* by Wayne Grudem.[8] At first it may appear to be an intimidating book, but as you read each sentence, page, and chapter you will find that it simply and concisely covers the doctrines of the Christian faith.

It is also wise for us to seek out mature Christians to disciple us. The best place to start is with our parents or pastor. If they cannot help us, they will be able to point us to someone who can.

It is also helpful to study Scripture in groups. The momentum of a group studying together can help us persevere over time. It also provides a great context to discuss key points more deeply and to ask questions. Discussions often help our head knowledge sink into our hearts. If your pastor leads a discipleship group or discussion group, ask to be a part of it. Suggest *Bible Doctrine* as the curriculum for the group.

A Call to Action

Do you have a firsthand knowledge of the truths of Scripture? Are you committed to rigorously study the teachings of the Bible? Remember, the goal is to grow in your love for God. Your knowledge of God should always lead to greater affection for God. Strive to have a passionate knowledge of biblical truths so that the foundation of your life is resting on solid rock and ready to withstand any storm that you may face.

Commit today to:

√ Study and learn sound doctrine
√ Grow in your love for God as you study
√ Apply what you know to your daily life

Questions for Reflection and Discussion

1. What is doctrine? Why is it important to study biblical doctrine?
2. Why does the study of doctrine seem to intimidate some Christians?
3. What is the difference between firsthand and secondhand knowledge of biblical truths?

4. Why do church kids tend to have secondhand knowledge of biblical truths? Why is this dangerous?

5. What is the relationship between knowing biblical truths and applying them to your life? What is an example of a biblical truth that you currently apply to your life?

6. What does the Great Commission say about teaching others? How should this affect our pursuit of studying biblical truths?

7. What does it mean to watch your life and doctrine closely? What is one area in which you need to watch yourself closely?

8. In the section "A Look in the Mirror," what did you learn about your knowledge of key biblical truths? What did you learn about your application of doctrine to everyday circumstances?

9. Why is it important to be both knowledgeable and passionate about biblical truths?

10. Which doctrinal area would you like to focus on in the next few months? What can you do to study it? How can other Christians help you in this?

Sing a New Song

"Join All the Glorious Names"[9]

Join all the glorious names
Of wisdom love and power
That mortals ever knew
That angels ever bore
All are too poor to speak
Your vast and priceless worth
Too poor to set my Savior forth

Chorus
Jesus Your name is glorious
Our Prophet Priest and King
Jesus You're reigning over us
And forevermore
Your praises we will sing

Great Prophet of my God
My tongue would bless Your name
Through You the joyful news
Of our salvation came
The long-awaited news
Of every sin forgiven
Of hell subdued and peace with heaven

Jesus my Great High Priest
You shed Your blood and died
My guilty conscience seeks
No sacrifice beside
Your pure and precious blood
For all my sin atoned
And now it pleads before the throne

For more information on this song, go to www.growingupchristian.com.

Trust in the LORD with all your heart
and lean not on your own understanding;
in all your ways acknowledge him,
and he will make your paths straight.

—PROVERBS 3:5–6

Lord, help me to

- understand what it means to trust you.

- trust you in times of trial and times of prosperity.

- know why you are worthy of my complete trust.

- not trust in my own wisdom and strength.

9 BANKING ON GOD

LEARNING TO TRUST GOD

Best Friends

When my father woke me up on the morning of August 14, 1988, I knew immediately that something terrible had happened. I could see it in his ashen face. My mom and brother stood in the doorway behind him, their watery eyes staring right at me. The look on their faces, more than anything, drove me from early-morning grogginess to total and instant alertness. I sat up in bed. A hundred horrible, imagined possibilities flashed through my mind.

Tears welled in my dad's eyes as he sat on the edge of my bed. I held my breath in anticipation, afraid to ask. After a seeming eternity, he choked out the terrible words. "Trevor has been in a really bad car accident. He didn't make it."

For a moment, the full reality didn't hit me. I pictured Trevor lying in a hospital bed, injured but still joking with the nurses and doctors, complaining about hospital food, and aching to get outside to shoot a few hoops. Then the rest of my father's words caught up with me, and my stomach lurched. It felt like the floor had just disappeared from beneath me. I fell back onto my pillow and closed my eyes in the sudden confusion and despair.

Not Trevor. Not my best friend.

Trevor and I had been inseparable from the time we were toddlers growing up on the same rural New Hampshire road. For as long as I could remember, we'd been playing together: battling imaginary spiders or battalions of ferns in the forest behind my house, challenging our older siblings to baseball or basketball, or just sitting around on rainy days playing Stratego or Monopoly. As childhood had given way to adolescence, our friendship had matured and strengthened. We carried our love of sports onto the court and ball field in middle school, where our previous years of teamwork and practice gave us an enduring ability to predict each other's moves and play off each other's strengths. Off the field, we spent countless hours discussing school, movies, and sports.

Our last conversation had been at Trevor's house three weeks earlier, the day before I left for a long family vacation. It was the summer before our senior year, and we spent a lazy afternoon hanging out in the sun, talking about our memories of the years gone by and our hopes and dreams for the year ahead. It was a rich conversation, one of the best Trevor and I had ever had.

And now, sitting in my bed surrounded by my grief-stricken family, I realized it was the last conversation we would ever have. I broke into tears.

As the days passed, we learned more about the circumstances of the accident. After a night of video games and bowling with some of his coworkers, Trevor had caught a ride with one of his buddies back to the restaurant where he'd left his car parked. The two were traveling too fast over a narrow, twisting back road, and they failed to make a turn. Despite having their seat belts on, they were both killed instantly.

In the days and weeks after the accident, sadness and confusion grew in my heart. I didn't understand why God had allowed Trevor to die. I knew that Trevor was a Christian, I knew Romans 8:28, and I knew that God promises to work all things for good for Christians, but I didn't see how this was good. I'd recall Ephesians 6:1–3, where

God says that those who honor and obey their parents will enjoy long life. I knew Trevor well, and he'd honored and obeyed his parents, but he died at the age of 17. I asked, "Why, Lord?" but I didn't get an answer.

I firmly believed God was in control, but I wanted to know why he had let my best friend die. As I mourned, I took long walks in the woods, visited Trevor's grave, and recounted the many great memories we had together. Many days I returned to the question, "Why, Lord?" Initially I was asking for an explanation, but my question grew to a dangerous demand for God to justify himself to me.

I knew I was headed down a slippery slope, and I realized that I needed to lay down my demands and trust God. Over time I began to notice a surprising change in my heart. Instead of becoming angrier, I found myself experiencing a growing sense of peace. Though God wasn't fully answering my questions, I felt him gently comforting me.

God spoke to me through Isaiah 55:8–9, which states that his ways and thoughts are higher and better than mine. He gave me faith to believe that he does work all for good, even if I didn't see the good. He enabled me to trust him and his promises, even though I didn't know how Trevor's death fit into his sovereign plan for Trevor, Trevor's family, or my life.

I still don't know exactly why God took Trevor to be with him in August of 1988. I do know that God used it to teach me the importance of trusting him, no matter the situation. He used it to give me a greater faith in him, and for that I am grateful.

It's Hard to Trust

Standing on the edge of the five-foot-high platform, Luke wondered if his teammates would catch him as he fell backwards off the platform and into their hands. His eyes were covered, but he could hear his teammates encouraging him

> **THINK ABOUT IT**
> And we rejoice in the hope of the glory of God. Not only so, but we also rejoice in our sufferings, because we know that suffering produces perseverance; perseverance, character; and character, hope. (Rom. 5:2–4)

to fall back. Although his arms were folded across his chest and his back was to the group, he knew that the eight of them could easily catch him. The real question was, could he trust them?

Have you ever participated in a team-building activity like this? Each member of the group has to depend on his teammates as he falls backwards into their arms. It builds trust and unity in a group, but it is extremely difficult, even if you are the last person to go and you have seen everyone else safely caught.

It is hard to trust others, whether it is our parents, siblings, teachers, pastors, or friends. It can be especially hard to trust God because we cannot see him or hear his voice, but it is essential that we learn to totally trust him and his promises. It isn't enough to just know God or believe the gospel. To live the Christian life, we need to trust him; we need to rely on his character and power in every moment of every day. Whether we experience trials or blessings, we need to believe that God is wise, loving, and fully in control of our lives and our world.

I found it hard to trust God as I mourned Trevor's death, but the more I did it the easier it got. Every day I felt God enable me to trust him and his ways more and more.

The more we choose to trust God instead of our own understanding (Prov. 3:5–6) and the more we understand that he is faithful, loving, kind, all-powerful, and wise, the easier it is to trust him. As we trust him through difficult trials and important decisions, we will see his constant care, comfort, and guidance for us.

Our Tendency

Not only do we have the privilege of growing up in Christian homes, we also live in a wealthy country. We do not face many of the challenges that are common in this world. We eat three meals a day and have no experience with severe hunger. We live in safe and comfortable houses and do not know what it is like to be homeless. Most of us live in safe neighborhoods and do not fear crime or harm as we play in our yards.

The struggles we face are relatively simple compared to those of many other people in this world. If we get sick, our parents take us to the doctor. If we struggle in school, our mom or dad helps us study for the next test. If we need advice, we stroll into the kitchen and ask our parents for their counsel.

But even minor trials are opportunities to learn to trust God. When we have a big test in Spanish, gain an interview for a part-time job, suffer a sprained ankle, or have just been cut from the basketball team, we have opportunities to learn to trust our heavenly Father. It is through these types of situations that God prepares us for more significant challenges in the future. They provide the first steps in learning to trust God on our own.

The key is to make sure that we trust God. As church kids we often trust our parents, our pastors, our teachers, and ourselves more than we trust God. Because we seldom experience significant trials on our own, we tend to look to the godly individuals in our lives for support and guidance to the neglect of looking to God.

> **THINK ABOUT IT**
> Another pitfall we need to watch for is the tendency to trust in God's instruments of provision rather than God Himself. In the usual course of events in our lives, God provides for our needs through human means rather than directly. . . . But these human instruments are ultimately under the controlling hand of God. They succeed or prosper only to the extent God prospers them. We must be careful to look beyond the means and human instrumentalities to the God who uses them.[1] —JERRY BRIDGES

Don't misunderstand. Our parents, pastors, teachers, and friends are wonderful resources that God uses to help and guide us. We need to take full advantage of their wisdom and counsel. We would be crazy not to. But we must realize that God is the one we must ultimately trust and that God is the one who directs and leads. He uses many different means to do this—the Holy Spirit, the Bible, and godly individuals in our lives—but he controls them all.

In chapter 6 we talked about developing our own convictions. That becomes especially important when it comes to trusting God. When trials come, our parents' faith won't give us enduring trust in God. Likewise, we can't look to the godly adults in our lives to carry us through every trial. Only God can do that. Trust has to spring from the depths of our own convictions about him. We can be confident that God will use our parents and other godly individuals to help us, but we have to learn to ultimately trust God himself.

The goal of this chapter is to help us learn why God is worthy to be trusted and how to trust him in every circumstance of life.

Take His Word for It

Joseph

The story of Joseph, recorded in Genesis chapters 37–50, illustrates how God is firmly in control even when the difficult circumstances of life may indicate otherwise. Joseph learned that God controls everything, despite Joseph's wrangling with pride, being sold into slavery by his brothers, suffering the lies of Potiphar's wife, rotting in prison, being forgotten by the cupbearer, and enduring years of famine in Egypt.

> **THINK ABOUT IT**
>
> Joseph powerfully testifies to God's sovereignty when he speaks to his brothers:
>
> You intended to harm me, but God intended it for good to accomplish what is now being done, the saving of many lives. (Gen. 50:20)

Despite incredibly trying circumstances over many years, Joseph learned that God is faithful, that his ways are the best ways, and that his purposes will be accomplished. He learned to trust God.

I'm sure my attitude would have been quite different from Joseph's. I probably would have doubted God all along the way, struggling with anger and the temptation to turn my back on God. I can learn a lot from Joseph's example.

Can you imagine the faith and excitement that Joseph experienced when he became second-in-command of all of Egypt? Can you picture his face when he realized that his family was standing in front of him and he had opportunity to sell them the food they needed to survive? Joseph must have laughed with joy as he finally understood God's purpose and plan. He must have cried tears of gratefulness as he saw how God had used him to save so many, including his own family (the future nation of Israel), from starvation. By persevering in times of trials, Joseph learned what it meant to trust God.

A God We Can Trust

The Bible makes it clear that God is great and worthy of our complete trust. We can totally depend on his character and power.

Consider a few of his many attributes:

> **THINK ABOUT IT**
> The Christian's instincts of trust and worship are stimulated very powerfully by knowledge of the greatness of God. [2]—J. I. PACKER

1. He is perfectly wise and all-powerful.

In your hands are strength and power to exalt and give strength to all. (1 Chron. 29:12b)

To God belong wisdom and power; counsel and understanding are his. (Job 12:13)

"For my thoughts are not your thoughts, neither are your ways my ways," declares the LORD. "As the heavens are higher than the earth, so are my ways higher than your ways and my thoughts than your thoughts." (Isa. 55:8–9)

Wisdom without power would be pathetic . . . [and] power without wisdom would be merely frightening; but in God boundless wisdom and endless power are united, and this makes him utterly worthy of our fullest trust. [3] —J. I. Packer

2. His love never fails.

Who shall separate us from the love of Christ? Shall trouble or hardship or persecution or famine or nakedness or danger or sword? . . . For I am convinced that neither death nor life, neither angels nor demons, neither the present nor the future, nor any powers, neither

159

height nor depth, nor anything else in all creation, will be able to separate us from the love of God that is in Christ Jesus our Lord. (Rom. 8:35–37)

It is the self-giving of God in the gift of his Son which convinces us that he will withhold nothing from us that we need, and allow nothing to separate us from his love. . . . So between the cross, where God's love and justice began to be clearly revealed, and the day of judgment when they will be completely revealed, it is reasonable to trust in him. . . . The cross does not solve the problem of suffering, but it supplies the essential perspective from which to look at it.[4] —John Stott

3. *He is completely in control of everything.*

For you created my inmost being; you knit me together in my mother's womb. . . . Your eyes saw my unformed body. All the days ordained for me were written in your book before one of them came to be. (Ps. 139:13, 16)

In him we were also chosen, having been predestined according to the plan of him who works out everything in conformity with the purpose of his will. . . . (Eph. 1:11)

In him all things hold together. (Col. 1:17)

4. *He never changes.*

In the beginning you laid the foundations of the earth, and the heavens are the work of your hands. They will perish, but you remain; they will all wear out like a garment. Like clothing you will change them and they will be discarded. But you remain the same, and your years will never end. (Ps. 102:25–27)

I the LORD do not change. (Mal. 3:6a)

Jesus Christ is the same yesterday and today and forever. (Heb. 13:8)

Which would you trust more as a lifeguard at your pool: a six-year-old who can barely swim or a twenty-five-year-old who has been a certified lifeguard for eight years and knows CPR? The choice is easy. We have a similar choice when it comes to trusting God or ourselves or anyone else. God's wisdom is infinitely greater than human wisdom. We should be quick to trust him over anyone and anything around us.

When we are aware that God is perfectly wise, all-powerful, loving, unchanging, and completely in control of everything, we will be better equipped to trust him. And these are only a few of his many attributes. He also never lies, knows everything, is everywhere at all times, is holy, is kind, and is good. God is worthy of our complete trust.

Our Response

What does this mean for us?

1. *We need to trust God instead of ourselves.*

Trust in the LORD with all your heart and lean not on your own understanding; in all your ways acknowledge him, and he will make your paths straight. (Prov. 3:5–6)

We need to start by trusting God and not our own understanding, experience, or wisdom. When we primarily trust ourselves, we proudly set ourselves up for a fall. When our confidence rests ultimately in our abilities, strength, and plans, we will stumble. But when we trust in the Lord with all our hearts and we acknowledge his control and his plans, we can count on him to make our paths straight, to guide us in what is right, and to lead us as we live our lives.

2. *We need to trust God and do our part.*

But we prayed to our God and posted a guard day and night to meet this threat. (Neh. 4:9)

Nehemiah supervised the rebuilding of the walls of Jerusalem after the exile. As the Israelites began to repair the walls, neighboring enemies heard and didn't want the project to be completed. They feared that the fully fortified city would allow the Jews to regain their strength. With the threat looming, Nehemiah had a choice: trust God or trust his own plan. He wisely chose both. The Israelites prayed to God, and they posted guards as others worked.

We can learn a lot from Nehemiah's example. Trusting God doesn't give us an excuse to idly sit back, doing nothing. Praying to God and asking him to help doesn't allow us to be lazy. We need to trust God and do our part in the strength and guidance he provides.

3. We need to trust God in trials.

> And we know that in all things God works for the good of those who love him, who have been called according to his purpose. (Rom. 8:28)

> Consider it pure joy, my brothers, whenever you face trials of many kinds, because you know that the testing of your faith develops perseverance. Perseverance must finish its work so that you may be mature and complete, not lacking anything. (James 1:2–4)

It is hard to consider trials pure joy, but there is a reason for this. Trials test our faith, develop our perseverance, make us more mature, and help complete us. When we understand that God uses difficult circumstances to build our faith, we will more easily consider them with joy. When we know that God works all things for good for Christians, we will trust him even when we do not yet see the good or God's purpose.

God taught me this key lesson through the death of my best friend, Trevor. He used the severe trial to build my faith, teach me perseverance, and make me more mature.

We don't always see the lesson, but we can be confident that God is at work in difficult times.

Perhaps he means to strengthen us in patience, good humor, compassion, humility or meekness, by giving us some extra practice in exercising these graces under especially difficult conditions. Perhaps he has new lessons in self-denial and self-distrust to teach us. Perhaps he wishes to break us of complacency, or unreality, or undetected forms of pride and conceit. Perhaps his purpose is simply to draw us closer to himself in conscious communion with him.[5] —J. I. Packer

4. We need to trust God for the future.

In his heart a man plans his course, but the LORD determines his steps. (Prov. 16:9)

"For I know the plans I have for you," declares the LORD, "plans to prosper you and not to harm you, plans to give you hope and a future." (Jer. 29:11)

He who began a good work in you will carry it on to completion until the day of Christ Jesus. (Phil. 1:6)

As we learn to trust God in day-to-day life and in current trials, we will learn to trust him for the future. If we lean on our wisdom and abilities, we will be anxious about the future. But if the infinite, eternal, wise, all-powerful, and loving God is determining our steps, we can look to the future with excitement. When we know he has plans to prosper us, we will more easily trust him for future events such as college, career, and marriage. When we understand that he will complete the work he has begun in our hearts, we can know that he will help us grow in holiness and defeat patterns of sin in our lives.

Knowing the character and promises of God, we can fully trust him for tomorrow, next week, next year, and the rest of our lives.

A Look in the Mirror

We have considered the character of God and discussed the importance of trusting him in every aspect of life. Let's turn now to see how we are doing.

First, let's consider the many situations God provides for us to learn to trust him.

WHAT'S THE OPPORTUNITY?

What is the opportunity you have to trust God when . . .

1. You have to study for and take final exams?

2. You are babysitting the neighbor's children and the two-year-old throws up?

3. You have to give an oral presentation in history class?

4. You are trying out for the varsity football or volleyball team?

5. You get cut from the basketball team?

6. You fall and break your wrist?

7. You fail a math test?

8. You don't get accepted by the college you want to attend?

9. School is difficult for you, and no matter how hard you try you cannot get good grades?

10. You don't have many friends at school?

Note: Possible answers are listed at the end of the chapter.

Those of us who have grown up in Christian homes may not have experienced the types of significant trials that many others in our world face, but we do face some challenges. It is important for us to see and seize the opportunities we have to trust God. Were you able to identify the opportunities to trust God in the situations listed above?

Second, let's consider whom we primarily trust: ourselves, others, or God.

WHOM DO YOU TRUST?

Rate yourself on a scale of 1 to 10. *1 means that you strongly disagree and 10 means that you strongly agree.*

MYSELF

____ 1. When I get sick with the flu or a cold, I focus mostly on what I need to do to get better (take medicine, sleep, drink tea or water, etc.) and forget to ask God to help me.

____ 2. When I have a big test or exam coming up, I focus primarily on my studying and my learning and forget to ask God to help me.

____ 3. When I think of the future (college, career, marriage, etc.), I become nervous, but I don't pray much about it.

____ 4. In trials or hard times, I often wish I were in control or I think I would do things differently if I were God.

OTHERS

____ 5. When I need advice in making a decision, I'm quick to go to my parents, but I often do what they suggest without much prayer.

____ 6. When I need counsel regarding a conflict with a friend, I quickly go to other friends and do not consider what the Bible says I should do.

____ 7. When I need academic help, I quickly go to my teachers or my smarter friends and ask them for help, but I do not also ask God to enable me to learn and understand as I go to them for help.

____ 8. In times of trial, I quickly seek comfort from my friends but rarely from God and his Word.

GOD

____ 9. I pray a lot in hard times and trials.

____10. I pray a lot when important events are coming up.

____11. I pray a lot when planning for the future.

____12. I think of my parents' advice as God's clear counsel to me.

____13. I think of the Bible as God's direction for my life.

____14. I often think about how God uses trials and suffering for my good, and I have known this to be true in my life and the lives of people around me.

____15. I get excited about the future because I know that God is in charge.

165

It is easy to trust people we know well and highly respect. We can and should trust our parents, pastors, teachers, and godly friends, but the key is to ultimately trust God as he uses them to help us. When we fail to see God as supreme, and we trust humans and human wisdom, trouble is lurking nearby.

Whom do you primarily trust?

Tips for Trusting God

Can we grow in our ability to trust God? Yes! Whether we are strong or weak in this area, we can learn to trust him more. Consider these five tips for growth:

1. Pray for faith and greater trust. In the Sermon on the Mount, Jesus taught his followers the importance of asking, seeking, and knocking (Matt. 7:7–8). He emphasized the kindness of God and his eagerness to answer our prayers. We need to be continually praying to God and asking him to fill us with faith and confidence in his promises. We need to call out to him, seeking to know his character and his ways. He is eager to answer our prayers, and he has given us the Holy Spirit to guide us as we learn to trust him.

If you want to grow in your ability to trust God, pray for greater faith and more trust.

2. Study Scripture to learn how trustworthy God is. We also need to study the Bible to learn about God's working in history, his plan of redemption, his character and ways, and his laws. The pages of Scripture are full of descriptions of our God. We need to study it with the goal of learning more about God's attributes and his ways.

I've included many Scripture references in this chapter. Go back and review them, look them up in your Bible, and let the power of the Word of God transform your heart and mind.

3. Study Scripture to learn how weak you are. We can also study the Bible to help us guard against trusting ourselves and leaning on our own understanding. When we study Scripture, we will learn how great God is and how limited humans are. This will protect us from trusting our wisdom and abilities and point us to God.

When we study about individuals such as King Saul, we will be reminded of our tendency to disobey and take matters into our own hands. When we read about King Nebuchadnezzar, we will see the dangers of pride and arrogance. When we read about King David, we will see him fail and repent, and we will also see God's faithfulness to him throughout his life. When we read the book of Romans, we will see how we all have sinned and need a Savior, and we will be reminded that nothing can separate us from the love of God.

The Word of God teaches us that God is strong and we are weak, and it should inspire us to trust God instead of ourselves.

4. Talk with Christians who have endured significant trials. Do you know anyone who has suffered from cancer? Do you know anyone who has lost a loved one as a result of serious sickness? Do you know anyone who has been out of work for years because of chronic pain? Do you know anyone who became paralyzed in a tragic accident? If they are Christians who are strong in their faith, you can learn a lot from them. Spend some time with them, and ask them how God met them as they persevered through their severe sufferings or trials. You will be inspired to do the same in your day-to-day life.

5. Read books about trusting God. We need to fill our minds with biblical truth on this topic. One helpful way is to read books that talk about trusting God.

Here are three that I highly recommend:

- *Trusting God* by Jerry Bridges.[6] It is a fairly simple book, yet it comprehensively teaches how to trust God. Bridges wisely explains that Christians easily trust God for salvation and going to heaven, but that we do not tend to trust God between these two significant events. His goal is to help Christians learn to trust God every day of their lives.
- *Knowing God* by J. I. Packer.[7] This outstanding book focuses on the doctrine of God. Packer discusses many of the amaz-

ing attributes of God and their significance to Christians and their faith. It is an inspiring book.

- *Bible Doctrine* by Wayne Grudem.[8] I recommend chapters 4–5, which focus on the attributes of God, and chapter 8, which teaches about the providence of God (how he controls everything). These chapters will elevate your view of God and give you confidence to trust him.

A Call to Action

God is worthy of your trust. It is vital that you trust him more than anything or anyone, especially yourself. Although God uses humans to help and guide you, ultimately he is the one leading you. Your parents, pastors, and teachers are tools that God uses to help you. As you seek to overcome the normal challenges of life, strive to trust God as he uses people to help you.

Commit today to:

√ Study the Word of God to learn more about the attributes of God

√ Pray and ask God to help you trust him above all else

√ Not trust your own wisdom or abilities

√ Seek to grow in your ability to trust God

Questions for Reflection and Discussion

1. What does it mean to trust God?

2. Why is it easier to trust ourselves than to trust God?

3. Why is it easier to trust our parents, pastors, teachers, and friends than to trust God? Why is this dangerous?

4. How are your parents, pastors, teachers, and friends instruments that God uses to guide you?

5. Why is God worthy to be trusted? What attribute of God gives you the most confidence to trust him? Why?

6. When do you find it hardest to trust God?

7. Why should we trust God in trials?

8. Can you think of a time in your life when God clearly used a trial for your good? What happened?

9. In the section "A Look in the Mirror," what did you learn about yourself in the first chart? The second chart?

10. What is one current situation in your life in which you have an opportunity to trust God?

11. Which of the five tips would you like to work on in the next month?

Sing a New Song

"O Wondrous Love"[9]

O wondrous love that will not let me go
I cling to You with all my strength and soul
Yet if my hold should ever fail
This wondrous love will never let me go

O wondrous love that's come to dwell in
     me
Lord who am I that I should come to know
Your tender voice assuring me
This wondrous love will never let me go

Chorus
I'm resting in the everlasting arms
In the ever faithful heart
The Shepherd of my life
You carry me on Your mighty wings of
     grace
Keeping me until the day
I look into your eyes

O wondrous love that sings of Calvary
The sweetest sound the sinner's ever known
The song of your redeeming Son
Whose wondrous love will never let me go

O wondrous love that rushes over me
I can't escape this river's glorious flow
You overwhelm my days with good
Your wondrous love will never let me go

For more information on this song, go to www.growingupchristian.com.

POSSIBLE ANSWERS TO:
WHAT'S THE OPPORTUNITY?

You can trust God that:

1. He will give you enough time, energy, and perseverance to study, and he will help you remember all that you study.

2. He will enable you to clean up, care for, and comfort the child, and assure you that the child will be okay.

3. He will help you prepare a good presentation, do your best, not fear the opinion of your classmates, be calm and speak clearly, and say everything you plan to say.

4. He will help you do your best in keeping up with the rest of the individuals trying out. If you get cut, still believe that he is good.

5. He will help you believe that he didn't want you to be on the team this year, work hard and try again next year, and know that your worth and identity are not determined by the team.

6. He will heal you, not allow permanent damage, and give you patience as you wait to heal.

7. He will help you learn the material, study more effectively, and do better on the next test.

8. He wants you to go to another college, has a different and better plan for you, and is wise and knows what is best for you.

9. He wants you to do the best you possibly can and doesn't just evaluate you by your grades, will help you persevere even when you don't see all the results you want from your hard work, and won't let you become discouraged.

10. He controls your friendships, will provide the right friends for you, will help you to reach out to others, is your closest friend, and is always present to comfort and help you.

PART **3** LIVING BIBLICALLY

For if you live according to the sinful nature,
you will die; but if by the Spirit you put to death
the misdeeds of the body, you will live. . . .

—ROMANS 8:13

Lord, help me to

- understand your perfect holiness.

- see my sin as you see it and hate my sin as you hate it.

- live according to your Word.

- battle the sinful motives and desires that drive my wrong actions.

10 THE FIGHT OF YOUR LIFE

BATTLING SIN

Life or Death

If help didn't come soon, Aron Ralston was going to die. For five straight days, his anguished body had been exposed to the brutal desert climate. He had no food, and had run out of water two days earlier. The painful, intense thirst had driven him almost to the point of madness. His tongue had grown thick and swollen in his mouth. He drifted in and out of delirium.

Aron gathered his strength to make a final cry for help. The hoarse, pitiful croak that emerged from his mouth sounded frighteningly inhuman. It echoed back through the canyon, almost mocking his aloneness. No one would be within twenty miles of here. You'd have to be crazy to venture this far out into the rocky wild. That, or be a canyoneer. Both of which amounted to the same thing, Aron mused darkly.

It was Utah's vast, beautiful, winding canyons that had brought him here. An experienced mountaineer from Aspen, Colorado, he had turned his attention west for an adventure in "canyoneering," an extreme sport entailing both hiking and climbing up and down steep, rugged terrain. Like many other outdoorsmen, Aron was a man who loved nature and valued solitude, and preferred to adventure alone. Though canyoneering alone through such barren territory gave one an unparalleled degree of peace and quiet, it was decidedly more dangerous than going with a partner. If anything happened, help was a long, long way away.

Aron understood that all too well. He looked down at his right arm, which was crushed against the canyon wall by a boulder almost as large as he was. The accident had happened the day he set out, on April 26, 2003. He'd been climbing over the boulder in a three-foot-wide section of Bluejohn Canyon when the boulder suddenly shifted, slamming him against the wall and pinning him in place. For more than five days now he had fought, twisted, and pried to free his trapped arm, but the boulder hadn't shown the slightest sign of moving. He was its prisoner.

Not anymore, Aron knew. He would die if he stayed here, and it was clear that help wasn't coming. He'd been thinking about his last, most desperate option for several days now. The time for action had finally come. It would be terrible, but the alternative was death.

With his left hand, Aron managed to fish out his pocketknife and open the flimsy blade. His heart was thundering now, but he had a calm, almost peaceful knowledge that this was what he had to do. He took one final, deep breath, then brought the blade to his right forearm and began to saw.[1]

Aron Ralston had to make an incredible decision, but he knew it was the only way he would survive. Amputation was a drastic move, but the alternative was death. Aron was willing to do whatever it took to save his life. His determination paid off. After the crude amputation, he set up a rappel with his one free hand, descended to the desert floor, and hiked to safety.

Christians face a similar decision when it comes to fighting their sin. Paul said, "For if you live according to the sinful nature, you will die; but if by the Spirit you put to death the misdeeds of the body, you will live . . ." (Rom. 8:13). And in the Sermon on the Mount, Jesus said:

> If your right eye causes you to sin, gouge it out and throw it away. It is better for you to lose one part of your body than for your whole body to be thrown into hell. And if your right hand causes you to sin, cut it off and throw it away. It is better for you to lose one part of your body than for your whole body to go into hell. (Matt. 5:29–30)

The Word of God makes it clear that Christians should hate sin and love holiness. We must take seriously our battle against the sin of our hearts because if we live according to our sinful natures, we will die and face eternity in hell, but if with the help of the Holy Spirit we fight our sin and put it to death, we will find life and enjoy eternity in heaven.

Christianity is a fight. Christians are soldiers in a battle zone with an enemy nearby. We do not earn our salvation by fighting our sin, but we prove our faith to be true as we fight it. A genuine believer will live according to Paul's exhortation to fight the good fight of the faith.

THINK ABOUT IT

Fight the good fight of the faith. Take hold of the eternal life to which you were called when you made your good confession. (1 Tim. 6:12)

The true Christian is called to be a soldier, and must behave as such from the day of his conversion to the day of his death. He is not meant to live a life of religious ease, [laziness], and security. He must never imagine for a moment that he can sleep and doze along the way to heaven, like one traveling in an easy carriage. . . . If the Bible is the rule of his faith and practice, he will find his course laid down very plainly in this matter. He must "fight."[2] —J. C. RYLE

What about you? Do you live like a Christian soldier? Do you hate sin and love holiness? Do you vigorously fight your sin, or do you live according to your sinful nature?

Our Tendency

Why do we work to improve our academic and athletic skills more than we do to improve our relationship with God, especially battling our sin? If we fail on the basketball court or in math class, we usually make immediate plans to work harder, get help, and get better. We strive to improve no matter how much time, energy, or money it takes. We vigorously seek to eliminate our weaknesses, particularly when it affects how others think of us. Why do we work harder on our "public" weaknesses than we do on addressing the sins of our hearts?

Church kids know a lot about sin. Having been taught the standards of Scripture our whole lives, we know what we should and shouldn't do. We feel bad when we disobey God or our parents, and we know that our parents will discipline us when they learn of our sin. We try to change to avoid guilt and punishment, but our resolve doesn't seem to last.

Church kids tend to make five critical mistakes in battling sin:

1. We do not take our sin as seriously as we should. When we underestimate the seriousness of our sin, we battle it with little or no effort, or we do the bare minimum necessary to not feel guilty or not get in trouble.

2. We wrongly categorize sin as "major or "minor." We think of actions such as swearing, lust, drugs, getting drunk, and sex outside of marriage as major sins, and we consider sins like impatience, gossip, anxiety, and lying to be minor. Then we assume that we need to focus only on the major sins, and we overlook minor sins altogether.

3. We lack perseverance in battling our sin. We may start by working hard to fight our sin, but we often lack endurance in the battle. When we feel especially convicted about a sin, it's easy to gather our strength to fight it. Over time, though, it's easy for our resolve to weaken, especially if we stumble along the way. Soon we can give up altogether. It is difficult for us to battle our sin with determination and perseverance over a prolonged period.

4. *We battle our sinful actions, but we fail to deal with our sinful hearts.* It is easy to stop doing sinful actions yet fail to confront the sinful cravings of our hearts. This is especially true if we want to avoid the negative consequences of our sin. We can seek to eliminate our sinful behavior, but not address the sinful motives that drive the action.

5. *We confuse godly and worldly sorrow.* We typically feel bad when we are caught in our sins, when our parents correct us, and when we experience discipline. We can wrongly think that feeling bad means that we have experienced godly sorrow that will lead to change. We fail to understand that godly sorrow results from knowing that our sin is primarily against God, and that worldly sorrow is simply feeling bad for the negative consequences that result because of our sin.

The battle against our sin is incredibly hard. To win this war, we desperately need the help of the Holy Spirit, the Word of God, our parents, and our friends.

Take His Word for It

Remember the Gospel

Before we go any further, we need to remind ourselves of the gospel, which we discussed in chapter 2. We can easily become discouraged when we think about our sinful nature and actions, but we need to remember that God has solved our "sin" problem. On the cross, Jesus Christ bore the punishment of God for all our sins. When we place our faith in the finished work of Jesus, God completely forgives us and credits us with the perfect righteousness of Christ. Every sin we have ever committed, are currently committing, or will ever commit has been fully paid for. There is no reason to become discouraged when we look at our sin. Instead, we should

THINK ABOUT IT
This struggle against the sin in our heart is precious because by it we learn what a great price the Lord Jesus has paid. It is in this struggle that we will learn to trust Him and to distrust ourselves, to hate sin and love holiness, to cultivate humility and to long for heaven. And in the midst of it all, we'll learn the joy of obedience and the happiness that is found only in loving God.[3] —ELYSE FITZPATRICK

rejoice in the love, kindness, and forgiveness of God.

If you tend to condemn yourself and become quite discouraged when you think of your sin, mark this page so you can come back to it. The good news of the gospel needs to affect and control every aspect of your heart and mind. If you are a Christian, all your sins are paid for; Christ fully bore the wrath of God in your place. Remember the truth of Romans 8:1: "Therefore, there is now no condemnation for those who are in Christ Jesus. . . ."

The saving grace of God should encourage us, but we also have to guard against taking his kindness for granted. Being recipients of grace doesn't mean that we can live our lives however we want. A true Christian seeks to obey and glorify God in everything, and a genuine believer hates sin. John Owen said, "The choicest believers, who are assuredly freed from the condemning power of sin, ought yet to make it their business all their days to [put to death] the indwelling power of sin."[4] If God has done a work in our hearts, we should want to battle the sin of our hearts.

Christians are no longer slaves to sin, but that doesn't mean we

THINK ABOUT IT
Count yourselves dead to sin but alive to God in Christ Jesus. Therefore do not let sin reign in your mortal body so that you obey its evil desires. Do not offer the parts of your body to sin, as instruments of wickedness, but rather offer yourselves to God, as those who have been brought from death to life; and offer the parts of your body to him as instruments of righteousness. For sin shall not be your master, because you are not under law, but under grace. (Rom. 6:11–14)

are done with it. Although sin no longer rules us, we still are naturally sinful. God considers us righteous and credits us with the spotless record of Christ, but we still do sin. In fact, the battle with our indwelling sin starts at our conversion. Through justification we are declared righteous, and it is at this point that our sanctification—our growing in holiness—begins.

If we have been saved, we have been brought from death to life. This should change our motives and our actions. No longer slaves to sin, we can stop using our bodies to sin and begin to use them for righteousness.

When God saves us, he changes our hearts, motives, and goals. Although our sinful nature is still with us, we begin to resist sinful cravings and wholeheartedly pursue godliness. It isn't simple, but it is essential. It is the fight of our lives.

Why Should We Battle Sin?

Before we get into the basics of *how* to battle our sin, we need to look further at *why* we wage this war. Having grown up in Christian homes, we find it easy to fight sin just to avoid punishment or appease our parents. We need to examine and, when necessary, adjust our motives for fighting the sin in our lives.

1. We must understand what sin is. A sin is any act, word, or thought that breaks a command or instruction from God. Our sin may affect those around us or may be directed against someone in particular, but we need to see that all sin is primarily against God.

When David repented to God for his sin of adultery with Bathsheba and having her husband Uriah killed in battle, he said, "Against you, you only, have

> **THINK ABOUT IT**
> Wayne Grudem and J. C. Ryle provide two helpful definitions for sin:
>
> Sin is any failure to conform to the moral law of God in act, attitude, or nature. [5]—WAYNE GRUDEM
>
> A sin . . . consists in doing, saying, thinking, or imagining anything that is not in perfect conformity with the mind and law of God. [6] —J. C. RYLE

181

I sinned and done what is evil in your sight . . ." (Ps. 51:4). David clearly sinned against both Uriah and Bathsheba, but he rightly understood that he primarily sinned against God. When we correctly identify sin first and foremost as being against God and his commands, we will take all our sin more seriously.

2. We need to understand that we are sinful by nature. Because of the fall, all humans are born with sinful natures. Having been raised in a Christian environment, we can mistakenly believe that we are good. Not remembering a time of rebellion against God or our parents, we can wrongly think we have good hearts. Yet the opposite is true. We are each sinful at our core.

Scripture clearly describes the human condition. In Romans 5:12 Paul explains that sin entered into the world through one man and that this sin has affected all. In Psalm 51:5 David states, "Surely I have been a sinner from birth, sinful from the time my mother conceived me." In Romans 3:9 Paul describes all as being "under sin," and in Romans 3:23 he states that "all have sinned and fall short of the glory of God."

But this shouldn't discourage us. We must remember that the first step in any battle is to know the enemy and to learn about its goals and tactics. Kris Lundgaard said, "The more you discover the power of indwelling sin, the less you will suffer its effects."[7] When we understand how serious our situation is, we will be motivated to go after our sinful hearts, not just our sinful behaviors. When we see the power of our indwelling sin, we will recognize its lies and be ready to bombard the desires of our hearts with the truths of God.

3. We must understand God's view of sin. God is perfectly holy and can have nothing to do with any sin. In fact, Romans 2:5–11 describes how God will one day righteously judge everyone. On unbelievers, he will pour out his wrath because of their unrepentant hearts. On behalf of believers, he has already punished Jesus for our sins. His holy character demands that he hate sin, judge sinners, and pour out his wrath on those who sin. When we realize how much God hates sin, we will grow in our hatred for it, too.

4. It is essential that we understand the effects of our sin. Sin separates us from God and grieves him. Sin requires a consequence and often results in discipline. When we understand the price Jesus had to pay on the cross, and that every sin affects God, our relationship with God, and us personally, we will seek to battle sin with vigilance.

5. We must understand the consequences of not battling our sin.

If you live according to the sinful nature, you will die; but if by the Spirit you put to death the misdeeds of the body, you will live. . . . (Rom. 8:13)

Sin aims always at the utmost; every time it rises up to tempt or entice, might it have its own course, it would go out the utmost sin in that kind. Every unclean thought or glance would be adultery if it could; every covetous desire would be oppression, every thought of unbelief would be atheism, might it grow to its head.[8] —John Owen

An invading army can sometimes be persuaded to put down its guns by being given what it wants. . . . Some people think they can quiet the flesh's rage the same way. So they look for ways to "gratify the desires of the flesh" (Rom. 13:14). This is to put out fire with gasoline. Sin won't quench the flesh, only stoke it.[9] —Kris Lundgaard

Sin has extreme goals, and giving in to it or failing to vigilantly battle it has serious consequences. But when we understand the stakes involved, we should be all the more determined to persevere in waging the war.

A Look in the Mirror

We have defined sin and examined why we must fight it. Now let's look directly at our lives to examine our *reasons* for fighting our sin,

183

our ability to *identify the desire* behind our sin, and our *methods* for fighting our sin.

WHY DO YOU FIGHT YOUR SIN?

Check any that apply to you.

I try to stop sinning so that:

____ I will be well respected by my friends.

____ I will be well respected by adults around me.

____ I will be popular at school.

____ My parents will be happy.

____ I won't get into trouble.

____ God will be pleased.

____ I won't have to feel guilty.

____ I won't be punished.

____ I can be happy.

____ I can earn more privileges.

____ I can be thought of as a leader.

____ I can live according to the standards of the Bible.

Our reasons for fighting sin are important. The motives listed above are not all necessarily wrong, as long as we primarily desire to please God. But it is possible to try to stop sinning for the wrong reasons. When we are mostly concerned with avoiding discipline or becoming popular, we may change for a time, but it will not be a genuine change of heart, and it will not please God. To truly change and consistently want to flee from sin and pursue holiness, we must want to love, obey, and please God.

Now let's get practical. Can you identify the motive or desire behind a sinful behavior?

IDENTIFY THE MOTIVE

List possible wrong motives, desires, or cravings that could drive each sinful action.

1. Handing in a history paper that you copied off the Internet.
2. Sneaking out of your house in the middle of the night to hang out with your friends.
3. Listening to secular music that your parents wouldn't approve of and hiding it from them.
4. Lying to your parents about the people you talk with through instant messaging and the Internet.
5. Yelling at your sibling for coming into your room without your permission.
6. Slandering your science teacher as you talk with your closest friends.
7. Dating someone whom you know your parents will not approve of and hiding it from them.
8. Choosing not to speak up when your friends begin to gossip about a classmate.
9. Stealing a candy bar from the local convenience store.

Note: Possible answers are listed at the end of the chapter.

It may be easy to identify our sinful actions, but it is much harder and much more important to correctly identify the wrong desires behind our actions. How did you do in completing the chart above? Are you able to see and understand the motives of your heart?

Now let's consider the methods we use to fight our sin.

HOW DO YOU FIGHT SIN?

Rate yourself on a scale of 1 to 10. *1 means that you never do it and 10 means that you always do it.*

To fight my sin:

____ 1. I pray to God for help.

____ 2. I ask my parents for help and advice.

____ 3. I get counsel from my pastor.

____ 4. I read and study my Bible.

____ 5. I memorize Scripture verses relating to my sin.

____ 6. I talk with my friends.

____ 7. I find someone to hold me accountable to change.

____ 8. I read books that can help me.

____ 9. I promise myself that I won't do it again.

____10. I remind myself of the consequences if my parents find out.

____11. I listen to Christian music.

____12. I find a way to punish myself for my sin.

Do you use effective methods to battle your sin? Do you use all the people and tools God has given you? Do you view the battle against sin as the fight of your life?

How We Battle Sin

As genuine Christians, we should hate sin with such passion that we want to wage war against every sinful craving of our hearts.

So how do we effectively wage this war? Here are five tips to consider.

1. Pray to God for conviction of sin. We need God to help us to clearly see our sin and its seriousness. We need to pray that we see our sinful motives, desires, and cravings. We need to ask God to use the Bible, our parents, and our friends as tools to help us see our sin clearly. We should pray for God to give us genuine remorse for our sin. We need God's help to, first, see the sinful motives of our hearts; second, give us true conviction of and hatred for our sin; and third, help us change.

186

Do you pray for help? Do you pray that God will convict you of sin? Do you ask God to reveal areas of sin in your life? Do you ask God to help you hate a particular sin more than you currently do?

Prayer is the humble first step in the battle against our indwelling sin. It says, "I am taking sin seriously, I cannot do this on my own, and I need the help of God." When we pray for greater conviction of sin, God will give it to us, and we will be motivated to wage war against it.

2. Pray for help from the Holy Spirit. Just as a kindergartner cannot dunk a basketball without the help of an adult lifting him up, a human cannot battle sin without the help of the Holy Spirit. Battling sin is probably even more like a kindergartner's seeking to dunk on a million-foot-high rim. It is a humanly impossible task. But with the help of the Holy Spirit, our hearts can change. No longer slaves to sin (Rom. 6:17–18), we can resist temptation and find the way out that God always provides (1 Cor. 10:13). What is impossible on our own is now possible through the help of the Holy Spirit.

John Owen and Jerry Bridges remind us of the role of the Holy Spirit and our own role in this battle against our sin. They both use the term "mortification," which means to seek to put our sin to death.

> **THINK ABOUT IT**
> All other ways of mortification are vain, all helps leave us helpless; it must be done by the Spirit.[10]
> —JOHN OWEN
>
> Though mortification must be done by the strength and under the direction of the Holy Spirit, it is nevertheless a work which we must do. Without the Holy Spirit's strength there will be no mortification, but without our working in His strength there will also be no mortification.[11]—JERRY BRIDGES

We must rely on the strength and wisdom of the Holy Spirit as we fight our indwelling sin.

3. If we feel the conviction of the Holy Spirit but cannot identify the source of sin, we need to seek help. It is easy to identify sinful actions, but it can be difficult to figure out the wrong motives or cravings behind the actions. We must not hesitate to go to the many godly individuals in our lives—our parents, our pastor, and our mature Christian friends. We need to be humble, honest, and prepared to share our thoughts, words, and actions so that they can help us identify true motives of our hearts.

4. Once we have clearly identified the sin of our hearts, we need to repent and ask God to forgive us and enable us to change. Seeing our sinful behavior is good; identifying the sinful desires of our hearts is excellent; but neither is enough. We need to confess them to God and change.

First John 1:9 offers a great promise. God is faithful; God is just; God forgives; and God purifies. What an amazing God we have!

> **THINK ABOUT IT**
> If we claim to be without sin, we deceive ourselves and the truth is not in us. If we confess our sins, he is faithful and just and will forgive us our sins and purify us from all unrighteousness. (1 John 1:9)

5. We must battle our sin with the truths found in the Word of God. Once we have accurately identified the sin of our hearts and repented, we can begin to fight our sin. With the target in sight, we can utilize the truths and methods of the Word of God to fire torpedoes at the sinful cravings of our hearts.

The Bible contains the words of God and has great power. It is the primary tool that God uses to provide divine guidance and insight, convict sinners, change hearts, judge thoughts and attitudes, and train and equip Christians.

So how do we use God's Word to battle sin? Ephesians 4:22–24 teaches us to put off bad fruit and put on good fruit: "You were taught, with regard to your former way of life, to *put off* your old self, which is being corrupted by its deceitful desires; to be made new in the attitude of your minds; and to *put on* the new self, created to be like God in true righteousness and holiness." This passage provides a game plan for us. With the help of the Holy Spirit, we need to strive to *put off* all sinful desires and *put on* godly desires.

In the place of our sin, we are to put on new attitudes and new desires, and we should put on godly thoughts, words, and actions.

What does this look like in real life?

If we sin in anger because we were impatient with our younger brother, we need to put off impatience and anger and put on patience and kindness. If we sin in our speech by gossiping or slandering because we wanted to be accepted by the cool crowd, we need to put off ungodly talk and craving the approval of others, and we need to put on helpful and encouraging speech and seeking the approval of God. If we sin by cheating on a test in order to get a good grade, we need to put off laziness and deceit and put on hard work and honesty.

> **THINK ABOUT IT**
> All Scripture is God-breathed and is useful for teaching, rebuking, correcting and training in righteousness, so that the man of God may be thoroughly equipped for every good work. (2 Tim. 3:16)
>
> For the word of God is living and active. Sharper than any double-edged sword, it penetrates even to dividing soul and spirit, joints and marrow; it judges the thoughts and attitudes of the heart.
> (Heb. 4:12)

This isn't a magic pill to solve all our problems, but it is a game plan to apply to our daily lives. Through our efforts and the help of the Holy Spirit, we will see our need to change, want to change, and know how to change.

A Call to Action

We cannot save ourselves by putting off sin and putting on godliness. Only Jesus Christ who has paid the price for our sins can restore our relationship with God. Yet the life of a Christian should be marked by obedience and a deep desire to live in a way that pleases God. As we grow and mature in our Christian walk, we will get better at battling our sin and practicing godliness. We may not earn God's favor, but we must strive to please him more and more.

The battle against our sin is one of the greatest fights of our lives. With the help of the Holy Spirit, we can vigorously fight to the end.

Commit today to:

√ Hate sin as God hates it

√ Love holiness as God loves it

√ Seek to live in a way that pleases God

√ Examine the thoughts and motives behind your actions

√ Battle sin at the heart level

√ Depend on the help of the Holy Spirit to wage this war

Questions for Reflection and Discussion

1. Both Jesus and Paul made radical statements in Matthew 5:19–20 and Romans 8:13. According to their statements, why is it so important to battle sin?

2. What is sin? How do you know whether something is a sin? What is the difference between a sinful motive, a sinful thought, and a sinful action?

3. Why do church kids tend not to take sin seriously?

4. Do you categorize some sin as major and some as minor? Why is this dangerous?

5. What does God think of sin? Why?

6. What have you found to be the consequences of not battling your sin?

7. What did you learn about yourself in the self-evaluations? Why do you battle your sin?

8. Why is it hard to identify the motives, desires, or cravings behind our sinful actions?

9. What do you find are the most effective methods in battling your sin? Why?

10. How can the Word of God help in battling sin? How can your parents help in battling sin?

11. How does the Holy Spirit help us in battling our sin?

Sing a New Song

"Rock of Ages"[12]

Rock of Ages, cleft for me
Let me hide myself in Thee
Let the water and the blood
From thy wounded side which flowed
Be of sin the double cure
Save from wrath and make me pure

All the labors of my hands
Could not meet Thy law's demands
Could my zeal no respite know
Could my tears forever flow
All for sin could not atone
Thou must save, and Thou alone

Nothing in my hands I bring
Simply to Thy cross I cling
Naked, come to Thee for dress
Helpless, look to Thee for grace
To Thy fountain, Lord, I fly
Wash me Savior, or I die

While I draw this fleeting breath
When my eyes shall close in death
When I soar to worlds unknown
See Thee on Thy judgment throne
Rock of Ages, cleft for me
Let me hide myself in Thee

For more information on this song, go to www.growingupchristian.com.

POSSIBLE MOTIVES

1. Laziness, pride in having to earn straight A's, lack of fear of God.
2. Loving the world, lack of a desire to honor parents, deceit, fear of man.
3. Deceit, loving the world, seeking personal pleasure over honoring God and parents.
4. Lying, ungodly conversation, pursuing ungodly friendships.
5. Anger, impatience, selfishness.
6. Trying to impress your friends, fear of man, slander, gossip, lack of honoring authority.
7. Deceit, craving personal pleasure over honoring parents, lust, lack of self-control.
8. Fear of man, gossip, slander.
9. Selfishness, desire to impress friends, lack of fear of God.

Do not be deceived: God cannot be mocked. A man reaps what he sows. The one who sows to please his sinful nature, from that nature will reap destruction; the one who sows to please the Spirit, from the Spirit will reap eternal life. Let us not become weary in doing good, for at the proper time we will reap a harvest if we do not give up.

—GALATIANS 6:7–9

Lord, help me to

- grow in my love for you as I practice the spiritual disciplines.

- depend on the Holy Spirit in my disciplined pursuit of you.

- faithfully read and study your Word.

- find joy and life as I worship and pray to you.

11 SPIRITUAL PUSH-UPS

PASSIONATELY PRACTICING THE SPIRITUAL DISCIPLINES

Zacchaeus

Zacchaeus could hardly believe his ears when a merchant rolled into Jericho on his rickety cart, and casually mentioned to some bystanders curious for news that he'd passed Jesus of Nazareth on the road. The rabbi had been on foot, the merchant said, carrying little more than his sandals and robe, with an entourage of disciples in tow.

"What!" Zacchaeus exclaimed. "Coming here?" And before the startled merchant could answer, Zacchaeus set off at a run for the tax-collection office. He flew through the heavy iron door, a breathless explanation of the news already on his lips. "He's here," he said. "The rabbi is coming to Jericho." His stiff, rather unexpressive colleagues—who were bent over ledgers or counting denarii—just shook their heads and went about their work. They'd accused Zacchaeus more than once of being too excitable. When Zacchaeus saw that his enthusiasm was unshared, he said, "Well, I'm going out to meet him. I'll be back in a while. You may come along, if you wish." Then he went outside and hurried back to the gate.

Zacchaeus was dismayed to see that word was spreading throughout the city faster than he could have predicted. Hundreds of people were pouring into the open square inside the gate. Zacchaeus tried to squirm his way through the mob, but he was a small man, and the people in this city both knew and despised him. He was a tax collector, after all—in their eyes, a sellout to the Romans who willfully exploited his own people. When he tried pressing his way through the crowd, he was blocked and pushed aside.

Zacchaeus's heart sank. He had hoped desperately to see and hear Jesus for some time now. For months Zacchaeus had been living a life he hated, trapped in a job that he couldn't quite pry himself away from, but that invited the spite of both Jews and Romans. Everyone he had ever loved had long since walked away. What few friends he had remained loyal only because of his wealth. Even going to the synagogue was an oppressive experience, as he tried to comprehend a faith that seemed distant and remote to his experience, even as he endured the scathing looks from fellow worshipers. His life had come to ruins, but in the midst of his despair, Zacchaeus had heard about this man Jesus. He had met some of his followers, men and women transformed by a joy and zeal that he'd never seen before. Their passion had brought tears to his eyes. There was some great truth in this mystery that Zacchaeus wanted to know. But just on the threshold of meeting Jesus, he found his way blocked by an impassable crowd. Old Jericho's walls might as well be standing between him and Jesus.

He was beginning a lonely, sorrowful walk home when his eyes landed on one of the sycamore-fig trees wreathing the main street. It stretched nearly thirty feet tall, with thick, spreading branches. Zacchaeus spun to look back at the crowd, then looked up once more. He smiled with sudden determination. No matter what it took, he was going to see Jesus this day.

Climbing the tree was harder than he expected, and his clumsy efforts to navigate the branches brought laughter from passing citizens. A short, fat tax collector bumbling about in a tree was no doubt an occasion of great merriment for them. Zacchaeus ignored them and kept climbing, until he was safely nestled where he had an unobstructed view of the gate and the street.

Not long afterward, Jesus entered Jericho. He did not preach to the crowd, but it looked as if he was teaching his disciples as he walked. The crowd parted for him as he made his way down the street. People grew quiet to listen, even as hundreds of them reached out to touch his robe. Zacchaeus strained to hear, but Jesus was far away yet, and the rustling leaves in the tree seemed impossibly loud.

At last Jesus approached within earshot. He would pass directly beneath the tree. All of a sudden, however, Jesus stopped, folded his arms, and looked straight up at Zacchaeus with an amused smile. "Zacchaeus, come down immediately. I must stay at your house today." The sheer unexpectedness of it drove the crowd to silence. Zacchaeus felt himself blushing. Every eye in Jericho was on him. Yet any embarrassment he felt was overshadowed by the excitement surging through his veins. The Master had called him by name! He wanted to come into Zacchaeus's home! Zacchaeus scampered down from the tree as fast as he possibly could.

That was how his meeting with Jesus started. It was many hours later that they finally said their goodbyes, in the breaking dawn of the next day. Jesus walked away from Zacchaeus's palace-like house garbed only in his simple things, leaving a transformed man behind. Zacchaeus had found something precious and beautiful in the truth that the Christ had proclaimed. He had found the determination to make amends for the sins he'd committed, by repaying four times what he had exploited. Even more important, he had found salvation, and he had found meaning and purpose in his life. Zacchaeus had made every effort to see the Lord, and the Lord had met him.[1]

We can learn a lot from Zacchaeus. He desperately wanted to witness Jesus, so he ran ahead and placed himself in a position where he couldn't miss him. The result was more than he'd ever imagined: Jesus spoke to him, Jesus stayed with him, and Jesus transformed his life. Zacchaeus sought to simply see Jesus, but his initiative led to his complete transformation when he encountered the Messiah.[2]

197

Like Zacchaeus, we need to make daily decisions to place ourselves in a position where we can encounter God. As we seek the counsel of our parents, pastors, and mature Christian friends, God uses them to guide and direct us. When we attend a Sunday church service, small-group meeting, or youth conference, God uses the times of worship and teaching to speak directly to us. When we choose to go to people and events with a heart that anticipates meeting God, he faithfully transforms us into the image of his Son.

We can also position ourselves to hear from him in more private times. When we open the Bible and read it, God can speak powerfully to us. When we memorize a verse, God can empower us to change. When we pray and worship, we can experience the presence of the Holy Spirit. When we read excellent Christian books about key truths of our faith, we can grow in our love for God. And when we get away from the busyness of life and spend extended time alone with God, he meets us and builds our faith.

> **THINK ABOUT IT**
>
> God has given us the Spiritual Disciplines as a means of receiving His grace and growing in Godliness. By them we place ourselves before God for Him to work in us.[3]
> —DONALD WHITNEY

These private actions are called spiritual disciplines—specific practices that help us grow in our love for and knowledge of God. The spiritual disciplines, such as reading and studying the Bible, praying, worshiping, serving, fasting, and solitude, serve as spiritual exercises that strengthen our Christian walk. They are spiritual push-ups that build the muscles of our faith.

When we practice the spiritual disciplines with the goal of growing in our passion for God, we will see our love for him increase. When we faithfully practice them daily, we will see our walk with God strengthen more and more. When we regularly encounter the living God, he will be on our minds and guide us in each moment of our day. We will understand what it means to depend on the Holy Spirit and be determined to live in a way that pleases God.

The goal of this chapter is to help you understand the connection between practicing the spiritual disciplines and growing in your relationship with God. I desire to highlight the many blessings that result from a disciplined pursuit of God, and I hope to help you set in place specific practices that will lead to an ever-growing and ever-strengthening personal faith.

Our Tendency

Why do some Christians continue to grow in their faith month after month and year after year but others always seem to remain the same? I believe the difference lies primarily in their personal practice of the spiritual disciplines. Growing Christians are disciplined, regularly placing themselves before God and his Word.

If we all want to be like Christ, why don't we discipline ourselves? If we want to grow in holiness, why do we struggle to do the necessary work to accomplish this? I think this is due to five common tendencies:

1. We can forget why we should practice the spiritual disciplines. It is possible to read our Bibles and pray for the wrong reasons. We can even sing hymns of praise to God and evangelize the lost with the wrong motives. It isn't enough to simply do the right thing; we need to do the right thing with the right motive if we want to please God.

The purpose of practicing the spiritual disciplines is to grow in our love for and devotion to God. But we can wrongly do them to try

> **THINK ABOUT IT**
> Tom Landry, coach of the Dallas Cowboys football team for almost three decades, said, "The job of a football coach is to make men do what they don't want to do in order to achieve what they've always wanted to be." In much the same way, Christians are called to make themselves do something they would not naturally do—pursue the Spiritual Disciplines—in order to become what they've always wanted to be, that is, like Jesus Christ.[4] —DONALD WHITNEY

to earn God's approval, avoid his punishment, or gain his blessings. We can even focus on gaining knowledge of the things of God for the sake of appearing godly and impressing others. We can also complete our personal quiet times to avoid feeling guilty.

2. We can overlook the role of the Holy Spirit in our spiritual growth. If we seek to grow in our relationship with God totally in our own strength, we will find the Christian life to be all work and no play. If we seek to read the Word of God and understand it with our own wisdom, we will find it boring and lifeless.

Because spiritual growth requires us to work, we tend to focus only on our part. We can easily forget that growth in our walk with God requires us to depend on the help of the Holy Spirit. When this happens, we fail to ask the Holy Spirit to transform us as we pray, fast, and spend time alone with God. And when we do not ask the Holy Spirit to reveal the truths of Scripture or reinforce the biblical truths found in excellent Christian books, we will lack joy and life, and we will fail to regularly encounter the living God.

3. We can think that our discipline depends primarily on others. Working in our own strength is one extreme, but the other dangerous extreme is to depend primarily on others for our spiritual growth. It is one thing to pray when our parents ask us to pray, and another when we pray on our own. It is one thing to read our Bibles when we are asked to do so in Bible class, and another when we read the Word on our own. It is one thing to sing a Christian song during a youth meeting, and another to regularly worship God on our own. And it is one thing to contemplate truths of the Christian faith when our pastor asks us questions, and another to think about them on our own.

It is a great blessing to be surrounded by mature Christians who inspire us to grow in our walk with God. God definitely uses our parents, pastors, and Christian friends to help us grow in our faith, but we will not regularly encounter God unless we personally pursue the spiritual disciplines daily. It is our faith, our walk, and our Lord.

4. We can lack discipline over time. It is one thing to be disciplined for a week or a month, and another to live a disciplined lifestyle. If we want to be physically healthy, we need to be disciplined in how we eat and exercise, not only for a week or a month, but for our entire lives.

It is the same with our spiritual health. When we lack discipline in our pursuit of God, our spiritual growth will be inconsistent. When we lack perseverance and endurance, we will not grow over time. In fact, we may find our sin increasing and our faith lessening.

5. We can become too busy with other things. Life is full. Between attending school, completing homework, playing sports, having a part-time job, hanging out with friends, going to church events, and enjoying a little free time, our days seem to fly by. Many good things in life demand our time—now, today, this afternoon—and cannot wait. We wake up at 6:30 a.m. and go to bed at 11:00 p.m. Every moment seems full, and the thought of squeezing in thirty minutes to read our Bibles and pray seems impossible.

The urgent—instead of the important—rules our lives. Instead of being too busy to spend time with God, we need to realize that we are too busy not to. When we get too busy, even with good things in life, and we fail to regularly sow into our relationship with God, we will find ourselves overwhelmed and burnt out.

These may be five tendencies that church kids have, but they are not insurmountable. With God's help we can pursue him for the right reasons, depend on the Holy Spirit, learn to take responsibility for our spiritual growth, maintain a disciplined lifestyle, and ensure that spending time with God is one of our main goals for each day.

Take His Word for It

God grants us saving faith and he gives us the Holy Spirit to guide us as we live the Christian life, but he also calls us to "make every effort" (2 Peter 1:5), "train [ourselves] to be godly" (1 Tim. 4:7), "press on" (Phil. 3:12), and be "straining toward what is ahead" (Phil. 3:13). Scripture makes it clear that we need to intentionally strive for spiritual growth. To do this, we must be disciplined Christians.

In Scripture, God lays out some principles that will help us as we seek to faithfully and passionately practice the spiritual disciplines.

> **THINK ABOUT IT**
> For this very reason, make every effort to add to your faith goodness; and to goodness, knowledge; and to knowledge, self-control; and to self-control, perseverance; and to perseverance, godliness; and to godliness, brotherly kindness; and to brotherly kindness, love. For if you possess these qualities in increasing measure, they will keep you from being ineffective and unproductive in your knowledge of our Lord Jesus Christ.
> (2 Peter 1:5–8)

1. Our relationship with God is of first importance.

You shall have no other gods before me. (Ex. 20:3)

Jesus replied: " 'Love the Lord your God with all your heart and with all your soul and with all your mind.' This is the first and greatest commandment." (Matt. 22:37–38)

I consider everything a loss compared to the surpassing greatness of knowing Christ Jesus my Lord, for whose sake I have lost all things. I consider them rubbish, that I may gain Christ and be found in him. . . . (Phil. 3:8–9)

The primary objective of our quiet time should be fellowship with God—developing a personal relationship with Him and growing in our devotion to Him. . . . I like to think of the quiet time as a conversation: God speaking to me through the Bible and I responding to what He says.[6] —Jerry Bridges

2. Regular practice of the spiritual disciplines is essential for growth in godliness.

Do not be deceived: God cannot be mocked. A man reaps what he sows. The one who sows to please his sinful nature, from that nature will reap destruction; the one who sows to please the Spirit, from the Spirit will reap eternal life. Let us not become weary in doing good, for at the proper time we will reap a harvest if we do not give up. (Gal. 6:7–9)

One thing essential to growth in grace is diligence in the use of private means of grace. By these I understand such means as a man must use by himself alone, and no one can use for him. I include under this head private prayer, private reading of the Scriptures, and private meditation and self-examination. The man who does not take pains about these three things must never expect to grow. Here are the roots of true Christianity. Wrong here, and a man is wrong all the way through![7] —J. C. Ryle

3. We must depend on the Holy Spirit as we faithfully do our part.

If we are to make any progress in the pursuit of holiness, we must assume our responsibility to discipline or train ourselves. But we are to do all this in total dependence on the Holy Spirit to work in us and strengthen us with the strength that is in Christ.[8] —Jerry Bridges

God's Part:

For those God foreknew he also predestined to be conformed to the likeness of his Son. . . . (Rom. 8:29)

Being confident of this, that he who began a good work in you will carry it on to completion until the day of Christ Jesus. (Phil. 1:6)

203

Our Part:

> Train yourself to be godly. (1 Tim. 4:7)

> Pursue righteousness, godliness, faith, love, endurance, and gentleness. Fight the good fight of the faith. Take hold of the eternal life to which you were called when you made your good confession. . . . (1 Tim. 6:11–12)

> Do your best to present yourself to God as one approved, a workman who does not need to be ashamed and who correctly handles the word of truth. (2 Tim. 2:15)

When it comes to our physical well-being, we do not immediately see the effects of exercising or not exercising. If we stop exercising for a week, we probably will not see many effects on our health, but if we continue not to exercise for months and years, we will clearly see the effects. We will put on weight, lack energy, and quickly become tired.

The same is true with our walk with God. If we fail to sow into our relationship with God and stop practicing the spiritual disciplines for a week, we may not see the effects on our lives and hearts. But if we continue to neglect the spiritual disciplines for months and years, the effects will be drastic.

Roger Clemens pitches for the Houston Astros. It is no accident that he has over three hundred wins, has struck out over four thousand batters, and still pitches even though he is forty years old. He has one of the most rigorous and disciplined off-season workout programs of anyone in Major League Baseball. His discipline has allowed him to remain one of the best pitchers in baseball for over two decades.

Similarly, we need to rigorously discipline ourselves as we make every effort to pursue God and grow in godliness. Daily discipline coupled with the help of the Holy Spirit will result in strong and effective Christians who are passionate for God.

When we discipline ourselves and we faithfully sow into our relationship with God, we will find joy, peace, and life. We will see the benefits of a close and vibrant relationship with God, which will motivate us to sow into it all the more. That is the beauty of the spiritual disciplines: once we experience their rewards, we will be motivated to practice them more and more.

A Look in the Mirror

Now let's consider what we do to sow into our relationship with God, why we do it, and the fruit of our labors. Let's look at our practice, our motives, and the results.

PRACTICE

What do you do to deepen your relationship with God?

Check all that apply to you.

____ I regularly have a personal time alone with God.

____ I read my Bible.

____ I spend time thinking about key Scripture verses.

____ I memorize Bible verses.

____ I pray, asking God for help.

____ I pray, asking God to enable me to grow in godliness.

____ I pray, asking God to teach me as I read the Bible.

____ I occasionally get away for an extended time alone with God.

____ I spend time worshiping God in private.

____ I regularly serve others.

____ I regularly read Christian books that focus on key truths of the Christian faith.

MOTIVES

Why do you practice the spiritual disciplines?

1. Why do you read your Bible?
2. Why do you memorize Scripture verses?
3. Why do you pray?
4. Why do you have a personal time with God?
5. Why do you sing songs of worship?

6. Why do you serve others?
7. Why do you read books that focus on key truths of the Christian faith?

RESULTS

Rate yourself on a scale of 1 to 10. *1 means that you strongly disagree and 10 means that you strongly agree.*

___ 1. When I read my Bible, I know God is speaking to me.

___ 2. When I pray, I feel the presence of God.

___ 3. When I spend personal time with God, I find him guiding, directing, and encouraging me.

___ 4. When I get away for an extended time with God, I become more aware of how his Word applies to my life.

___ 5. When I worship God, I sense the presence of the Holy Spirit.

___ 6. When I serve others, I experience God's blessing and encouragement.

___ 7. When I read Christian books, I see that God is teaching me.

What did you learn about your current practice of the spiritual disciplines? What motivates you as you sow into your relationship with God? Do you find life and do you encounter the living God when you spend time with him?

Where Do We Go from Here?

What do we do if we want to grow in our relationship with God? We should do the same things we would do with any other relationship: look for ways to spend time together, talk with each other, make plans to bless each other, do things for each other, focus on each other's desires, try to get to know each other more, honor each other, serve each other, and enjoy each other.

If we want to grow in our love for and knowledge of God and live in a way that pleases him more and more every day, we need to sow into our relationship with him through daily prayer, worship, and

Bible reading. We need to consistently seek to grow in our knowledge of basic truths of the Christian faith by reading high-quality nonfiction Christian books, and from time to time we need to get away by ourselves for an extended time of solitude.

Let's look carefully at each of these five spiritual disciplines. But before we do, remember that the goal isn't to do each of these disciplines for its own sake; our aim is to grow in our relationship with God as we faithfully do them.

Reading and Studying the Bible

We need to read the Word of God daily. It is the story of God; it describes the character and nature of God; it outlines God's plan of redemption of mankind; it contains the inspired words of God; it is filled with truths that encourage us to believe and trust in God; it tells us about the promises of God; and it contains truths that will guide us as we live.

> **THINK ABOUT IT**
> No Spiritual Discipline is more important than the intake of God's Word. Nothing can substitute for it. There simply is no healthy Christian life apart from a diet of the milk and meat of Scripture.[9]
> —DONALD WHITNEY

It isn't enough for us to simply read our Bibles. We need to interact with God as we read Scripture. That is, we need to read our Bibles, think carefully about what God is saying, and seek to apply scriptural truths to our daily lives. The Bible isn't just any book; it is the very Word of the living God. He has given us Holy Scripture to teach and to help us, and we must open it and read it with reverence, anticipating that God has something to teach us.

It isn't enough to read through the Bible in a year. We need to read God's Word and take it to heart. And we need to make sure that we interact with all of Scripture—not just Psalms, Proverbs, and the New Testament.

I recommend that you place two bookmarks in your Bible, one in the Old Testament and one in the New Testament. Each day, with a pen in hand, sit down and read at least one chapter from each testament. As you read, look for any verse that jumps out at you and mark it with a star or underline it. When you finish the chapter, you may have one to three verses marked. Go back and reread them, think more about them, and ask God what he wants you to learn.

If you feel particularly affected by a verse, I encourage you to write down your thoughts in a journal. Write out the verse and the reference, and record what you are learning. Over the weeks and months, you will find your notebook filling up, and you will be encouraged as you read back through verses that God has used to help you grow.

Thinking carefully about a verse and journaling our thoughts is a practice called meditating on Scripture. It is an important part of understanding and applying the Word of God to our lives. It is helpful to read books of the Bible, but transformation of our hearts comes as we meditate on key verses of the Bible.

Another way to meditate on a Bible verse is to memorize it. Keep a supply of index cards near your Bible. If a verse really sticks out to you and you want to be sure to take it with you wherever you go, take the time to memorize it. Carry the card with you and review it throughout your day until you've committed the verse to memory.

Prayer

Jesus taught us how to pray (Matt. 6:9–13), told us to always pray and not give up (Luke 18:1–8), encouraged us to ask, seek, and knock (Matt. 7:7–11), got up early to pray (Mark 1:35), modeled how to pray (John 17:1–26), and in the Garden of Gethsemane prayed in preparation for his arrest and death (Mark 14:32–42). Jesus modeled prayer and expected his followers to pray.

The apostle Paul exhorted his readers to pray continually (1 Thess. 5:17), and he regularly prayed for them in his letters (Eph. 1:17–23; Phil. 1:9–11). The New Testament is filled with references to the importance of and need for prayer.

Prayer is communicating with God. Although he already knows our circumstances, thoughts, and needs, he expects us to pray. When we go to him for help or counsel, we humbly declare our need for him. When we ask him to heal someone, we acknowledge that he is

Lord over all. When we persevere in praying for the salvation of a family member, we declare that he is the source of saving faith.

Prayer takes our focus off ourselves and places it on our loving heavenly Father. It declares that he is great and that we submit to his power and his rule. We need to make prayer a key part of our personal times with God.

I suggest making a list of people for whom you want to pray. Keep the list manageable by breaking it up into seven different groups, and pray for one group each day. Record the list in your journal, and be sure to write down God's answers to your prayers.

We need to pray for others, and we need to pray for ourselves. We should be sure to pray for growth in godliness: humility, patience, greater passion for God, stronger desire to serve others, and increased love for the Word of God. We need to pray for help in overcoming temptations and battling sins, such as pride, selfishness, anger, laziness, and envy.

Prayer is a powerful tool that God uses to humble us and keep us dependent on him. He doesn't need us to pray, but he asks us to pray. He allows us to be part of accomplishing his purposes in our lives, our families' lives, and our world.

We need to faithfully and passionately pray each day.

Worship

Sometimes we can think of worship as something that we do as a group on Sunday morning or at a weekly youth group meeting. But Christians should seek to worship God in their personal times with him. We need to regularly worship God through music, whether we're singing, playing an instrument, or listening to worshipful CDs.

So many hymns and worship songs focus on key truths of the Christian faith. They highlight the character of God, the love of Jesus in dying for our sins, or how we can trust God in good and bad times. When we put these truths to music, they stick in our minds and transform our hearts. They come back to our lips throughout the day, and they encourage and inspire us.

THINK ABOUT IT
Music is a wonderful tool God has given us to express our affections for him. Psalm 100 expresses this so well:

Shout for joy to the Lord, all the earth. Worship the Lord with gladness; come before him with joyful songs. Know that the Lord is God. It is he who made us, and we are his; we are his people, the sheep of his pasture. Enter his gates with thanksgiving and his courts with praise; give thanks to him and praise his name. For the Lord is good and his love endures forever; his faithfulness continues through all generations. (Ps. 100)

One of the reasons we have included lyrics to hymns and worship songs at the end of each chapter is to help you worship God more effectively. I pray that the truths and melodies of these songs help you love God more and grow in your faith.

Be a Christian who regularly sings out in worship to your God during your personal times with him.

Reading Theological Books

Theology is simply the study of God. All Christians are theology students and should seek to learn as much as possible about God, his promises, and his commands. We can do this by studying the Bible and by studying works of theologians who have done their own study of the truths of Scripture.

As you grow as a believer, you should continue to read and add to your library of excellent Christian books. Christianity has a long spiritual and literary heritage from which we can draw. Here are a few suggestions to begin with:

- *Discipline of Grace* by Jerry Bridges
- *Knowing God* by J. I. Packer
- *The Truth and Grace Paradox* by Randy Alcorn
- *Spiritual Disciplines for the Christian Life* by Donald Whitney
- *The Cross-Centered Life* by C. J. Mahaney
- *Idols of the Heart* by Elyse Fitzpatrick
- *The Enemy Within* by Kris Lundgaard

Solitude and Personal Retreats

Sometimes life gets so busy that we need to set aside an extended period of time to seek God. Whether it be for three hours on a Saturday morning or an entire evening, we occasionally need to spend uninterrupted time with God to pray, get into the Word, journal, and worship him.

I recommend that every three months you set aside at least three hours to do this. Go to a local park or lock yourself in your bedroom and commune with God. You may even want to coordinate this time with your parents. You can all do an in-house retreat so that you won't disturb each other, or you could all go camping for the weekend with a block of time set aside for everyone to get alone with God.

When we have long, uninterrupted times with God, we will be able to seek him quietly and patiently. Without the rush of a busy morning and a full day ahead of us, we can wait on God, study Scripture, and pray to him.

During these times it is important to write down what God teaches you. You can review it in the weeks that follow and during your next time of solitude.

When we study God's Word, pray, worship, study theological books, and have times of extended solitude, we will grow in our knowledge of God and our love for him. When we faithfully and passionately practice these spiritual disciplines, we will see our faith grow. When we encounter the living God in these times, we will look forward to spending more time with him. Over time we will see ourselves become more and more like Christist.

A Call to Action

Personal holiness and growth in godliness do not happen by accident. Relying on the power of the Holy Spirit, train yourself in godliness. Discipline yourself to pursue your Lord and Savior. Strive to practice the spiritual disciplines with your whole heart.

Commit today to:

√ Grow in your love for and knowledge of God

√ Read and study the Bible

√ Faithfully pray

√ Consistently practice the spiritual disciplines with the goal of growing in godliness

Questions for Reflection and Discussion

1. What are the spiritual disciplines? What is the purpose of practicing them?

2. What hinders you from regularly practicing the spiritual disciplines? What can you do to overcome these hindrances?

3. What is our own role in our spiritual growth? And what is the Holy Spirit's role in our spiritual growth?

4. In the section "A Look in the Mirror," what did you learn about your motives in practicing the spiritual disciplines?

5. What results do you see in your life for your faithful practice of the spiritual disciplines? And for your lack of practice of them?

6. How often should a Christian teenager have a quiet time/personal devotion? What should a person do during a quiet time?

7. Why is reading and studying the Bible so important? Why is prayer so important?

8. What Christian hymns and worship songs do you find yourself regularly singing? How do these songs affect you?

9. What great books have you read recently that have strengthened your faith? What is one book that you would like to read in the next few months?

10. What is the difference between a time of solitude and a daily quiet time/devotion?

11. Where is a good spot you could go for three hours of uninterrupted time with God?

Sing a New Song

"Your Great Renown"[11]

Our hearts are longing for
The glory of the Lord
To be made known in all the earth
Lord, let Your kingdom come
Lord let Your will be done
Yours is the greatest name of all

Chorus
We want to see the nations bow
We want to hear the rising sound
Of the worship that You deserve
We want this passion to abound
A burden for Your great renown
For Yours is the greatest name of all

Our hearts are longing for
The wisdom of the Lord
To be proclaimed in all the earth
Your ways are higher than
The dreams of any man
Yours is the greatest name of all

Our hearts are hungry for
The power of the Lord
To be displayed in all the earth
The message of the cross
Will bring hope to the lost
Yours is the greatest name of all

For more information on this song, go to www.growingupchristian.com.

From everyone who has been given much, much will be demanded; and from the one who has been entrusted with much, much more will be asked.

—LUKE 12:48

Lord, help me to

- see my talents as gifts from you.

- faithfully steward my talents.

- use my gifts to serve you and to further your kingdom.

12 MAKING THE MOST OF IT

FAITHFULLY STEWARDING YOUR GOD-GIVEN TALENTS

Striving for Excellence

Those who knew Theodore Roosevelt as a young boy would never have imagined that he'd one day become the President of the United States. After all, a sickly, pale, asthmatic boy hardly seemed presidential material. Roosevelt suffered such severe asthma attacks, in fact, that he was often too ill to attend school. One day when he was twelve years old, his father called him into his office for some simple but stern advice: "You have the mind but you have not the body, and without the help of the body the mind cannot go as far as it should. You must make your body!"[1] Roosevelt took his father's advice seriously. Despite his affliction, Roosevelt possessed one quality that poised him for success his entire life: a fighting spirit that invested in the future. This spirit permeated every part of his life, from physical training to the cultivation of his intellect and the leading of the country.

Though circumstances were stacked against him, Roosevelt knew the power of discipline and practice, and from a young age exercised and trained his body. Over time, his investment paid enormous returns. What began as a strenuous course in calisthenics led to increasingly challenging physical accomplishments. In one phase of his life Roosevelt became a rancher, spending long hours in the saddle. On his honeymoon he climbed the Matterhorn, a demanding mountain that had claimed the lives of her first climbers. After his presidency Roosevelt spent a year hunting in Africa and went on a wilderness expedition to map the Rio da Divuda, a river in Brazil.[2]

Roosevelt's mind was naturally exceptionally sharp, but he exercised it with the same spirit of discipline and investment in the future. He learned from the tutors his parents hired. He loved to read, especially about history and science, and dreamed of one day becoming a scientist or engineer. His later contributions as a historian and naturalist were significant. Roosevelt's cultivation of his intellect led to opportunity after opportunity in his life. By the time he was forty-two, he'd served as a New York State Assemblyman, Governor of New York, Vice President, President, a deputy sheriff, a police commissioner, a U.S. Civil Service commissioner, and Assistant Secretary of the Navy. He wrote more than thirty-five books and over 150,000 letters.[3]

Roosevelt also invested in the future of the United States. One of his most lasting contributions to the world was the Panama Canal, which linked the Atlantic and Pacific oceans without the need to sail all the way around South America. He also took strides to ensure that America's beautiful wilderness areas would be protected. He designated one hundred fifty national forests, five national parks, and eighteen national monuments, along with other preserves and reservations. Altogether he provided federal protection for almost 230 million acres of land.[4] Americans today still enjoy the fruits of this effort.

Theodore Roosevelt lived one of the most remarkable and varied lives in American history. His achievements range from scientific to political, literary to physical. Though Roosevelt was gifted with a brilliant mind, that alone can't explain his amazing legacy. That can be explained only by his willingness to cultivate his talents from a young age and to make investments that would last a lifetime. Reading and study sharpened his already quick mind. By disciplined practice, he transformed his physical weakness into great physical strength. His foresight and vision affected America forever.

We as Christians can take a lesson from Roosevelt's example. Church kids in particular have been blessed with a wide range of abilities and resources. We have our own unique talents and abilities. We typically have a strong education in the Bible and a solid understanding of the Christian life. Many of us have wise, caring parents who encourage us to put our talents to use. We are poised for success—if we invest our talents wisely.

Roosevelt's father encouraged him to exercise his body so that it would complement his mind and so that he could put his talents to their fullest use.

> **THINK ABOUT IT**
> What would our Father say to us church kids if he summoned us to his own heavenly office? I imagine it might sound something like this:
>
> You have been taught well by your parents, pastors, and teachers; you have had the wonderful privilege of growing up in a loving Christian home; and you have a lot of potential. You know my Word and my commands, but I fear that you are not spiritually strong. You need to establish a rigorous practice of spiritual exercise and begin preparing today for the tasks I will call you to in the future.

God has blessed us abundantly with talents and opportunities, but the mere presence of those things doesn't guarantee success. Having gifts from God doesn't mean that we are spiritually strong. We can have them and not use them, or we can use them for our own glory instead of the Lord's. To run the Christian race well, we must wisely invest and exercise our talents.

We are stewards who have been entrusted with specific skills and abilities. This chapter focuses on how to be a faithful steward of our talents, preparing today for the purposes God calls us to, both now and in the future.

Our Tendency

Investing for Retirement

Consider the following chart. The first column represents the ages of 18 to 65. The other three columns represent the retirement accounts for three different investors. Scan down each column to see the account balance grow over the years.

Investment Chart

Age	Investor #1 ($0/month)	Investor #2 ($100/month)	Investor #3 ($100/month)
18	$1,000	$1,000	$10,000
20	$1,210	$3,730	$14,620
25	$1,948	$13,333	$30,871
30	$3,137	$28,799	$57,044
35	$5,053	$53,707	$99,196
40	$8,138	$93,823	$167,083
45	$13,107	$158,430	$276,415
50	$21,110	$262,479	$452,496
55	$33,998	$430,052	$736,077
60	$54,755	$699,929	$1,192,786
65	**$88,184**	**$1,134,569**	**$1,928,321**

Investor #1 started with $1,000 and earned 10 percent interest each year. Investor #2 is just like investor #1 except that he adds $100 a month from age 18 to 65. Investor #3 is just like investor #2 except that he starts with $10,000 instead of $1,000.

Glancing at the bottom row, it is staggering to consider the difference in each account at age 65. The chart illustrates two key factors in financial investment: monthly investment and initial investment. The more we invest each month and the more we start with, the more we will have when we retire. Although we don't like to think about it, there is a negative side to these principles: the less we invest each month and the less we have to start with, the less we will have at age 65.

This is also true when it comes to stewarding our talents. The more we invest in our talents on a daily basis, the more our talents will grow. And the more talents we start with, the more we will have as we seek to develop them. The choices we make today in managing our talents determine how effective we will be for God in the future.

As church kids, we are like investor #3, who had a large initial investment. Yet we can also tend to be like investor #1, who didn't add to the initial investment over time.

Throughout this book, I have pointed to the blessings of growing up in a Christian home. We have been raised in a rich Christian environment and have been taught many spiritual truths by our parents, pastors, and teachers. We have been encouraged to read our Bibles, and we have been instructed in the message of the gospel. We have learned about God's nature, his commands, and his promises. We have been taught how to pray and how to trust God. We have grown up with privileges that many people never experience in life and some encounter only after their conversion later in life.

> ### THINK ABOUT IT
> From everyone who has been given much, much will be demanded; and from the one who has been entrusted with much, much more will be asked. (Luke 12:48)

We are like a farmer on a state-of-the-art farm with acres of rich, fertile soil, modern equipment, huge fields, and established markets to sell the crops. But the farmer cannot rest upon the quality of his farm or the power of his equipment. He must put them all to work, faithfully tilling the soil, planting the seeds, and harvesting the crops. He needs to do the daily hard work of managing the farm if he is going to succeed.

As church kids, we have been given much, and much is required of us. We cannot rest on the privileges we experience. We cannot simply go with the flow and attend church, go to youth meetings, and read our Bibles just because our parents ask us to. We cannot give 100 percent effort to sports and music and invest our talents for God on the side.

We have to see ourselves as stewards: individuals who manage tasks or objects entrusted to them. We are Christian stewards in the service

> ### THINK ABOUT IT
> A steward manages assets for the owner's benefit. The steward carries no sense of entitlement to the assets he manages. It's his job to find out what the owner wants done with his assets, then carry out his will.[5] —RANDY ALCORN

of God. We are not on our own with independent gifts. We are God's managers, specifically responsible for overseeing our lives—our talents and possessions. Whether it is a car, clothes, money, or talents, we must understand our role in stewarding them for the glory of God.

To effectively steward our gifts and talents, we need to faithfully use them and look for ways to improve them.

Take His Word for It

Faithfulness

In chapters 24 and 25 of the gospel of Matthew, Jesus taught his disciples about the end times. In the middle of his teaching, he told the parable of the talents (Matt. 25:14–30). It is the well-known story of a master who called three of his servants to him and gave them talents, which was the currency of the day. Based on the ability of each servant, the master decided to give the first servant five talents, the second two talents, and the third one talent. Then the master went away on a long journey.

When the master returned, he again gathered his servants to find out what they had done with the money he had entrusted to them. The one who was given five talents had wisely invested them and earned five more, and the one who was given two had earned two more. But the third servant, who was given one talent, was fearful and had failed to invest the money. Instead, he had buried it in the ground so that no one could steal it.

The master was extremely pleased with the two servants who had doubled their money, but he was furious with the one who had done nothing. To the first two he gave great responsibilities in his kingdom, but he called the third wicked and lazy before having him thrown out of his kingdom.

Jesus told this parable to explain our roles as stewards in his kingdom. We have all been given different skills, gifts, and abilities that we are responsible for. God calls us to be faithful; he wants us to take our talents and look for ways to use and improve them. He wants faithful Christians who consistently strive to make a great difference in his kingdom.

As church kids, we are "five-talent" individuals. We have been given many gifts and abilities that we need to faithfully steward.

How will your Master rate your faithfulness when he returns?

Faithful in Little—Faithful in Much

Sometimes we can think we'll be organized and work hard when we get a really important job after college, but we fail to see that our organizational skills and work ethic today determine our future qualifications for significant responsibilities in the future. Sometimes we can miss the connection between who we are right now with who we will become later. We can overlook our current actions and wrongly assume that we will live differently when we need to.

Our daily effort in homework and studying affects our test grades. Our concentration in basketball practice affects our performance in a game. Our daily diet and exercise routine affect our physical health. Our practice of the spiritual disciplines affects our relationship with God. And our faithfulness in little things affects our ability to be faithful in bigger responsibilities.

Faithfulness in small things leads to faithfulness in larger things because (1) we learn how to be faithful through practice, and (2) people tend to give us greater responsibilities when they see us being faithful in other areas.

Your principal invites you to serve on the student council because

THINK ABOUT IT

In Luke 16:1–13, Jesus taught his disciples by telling them the parable of the shrewd manager. Using the example of managing money, Jesus illustrated a key principle of stewardship:

Whoever can be trusted with very little can also be trusted with much, and whoever is dishonest with very little will also be dishonest with much. (Luke 16:10)

he sees your positive leadership in your class. Your yearbook adviser asks you to be the editor because she sees your organization and vision and knows you are ready for the task. Your youth pastor invites you to be on the worship team because he has seen both your musical skills and your passion for God.

Faithfulness leads to greater opportunities, and a lack of faithfulness leads to fewer opportunities.

Are you faithfully stewarding your gifts for the glory of God?

Gifts from God

We may possess unique talents and abilities, but they are all gifts from God. Our minds, bodies, and abilities come from God. He entrusts them to us and asks us to use them for his glory. He wants us to work hard to develop our abilities and look for ways to accomplish his will with them.

The focus shouldn't be on us or our abilities; the focus should be on the source—God. When we understand this, we will give him the glory and look for ways to use our talents for him. Henry and Mel Blackaby wrote, "If we operate only according to our talents and

ability, we get the glory. But if we function according to the power of the Spirit, God gets the glory as others around us see Him at work."[7]

God is the source of anything and everything good in us. To him be the glory!

We Will Reap What We Sow

The first sentence of Galatians 6:7 is a wake-up call to everyone. We cannot afford to deceive ourselves. God's character, God's laws, and God's ways cannot be mocked. He knows when we act in a way that pleases our sinful nature, and he knows when we act in a way that pleases him. He makes sure that we all reap in a way that is consistent with our sowing.

> **THINK ABOUT IT**
> Do not be deceived: God cannot be mocked. A man reaps what he sows. The one who sows to please his sinful nature, from that nature will reap destruction; the one who sows to please the Spirit, from the Spirit will reap eternal life. Let us not become weary in doing good, for at the proper time we will reap a harvest if we do not give up. (Gal. 6:7–9)

This is a scary promise if we are sowing to our sinful nature, but it is a wonderful guarantee if we are sowing to the Spirit. When we use our talents for God's glory, we will surely reap a blessing from him. He will increase our gifting, give us more responsibilities, grant us great joy in serving him, and make us more effective for him.

Eternity on Our Minds

Faithful Christian stewardship requires long-term thinking. We need to think beyond this week, this month, or this year, and consider eternity. Yes, sowing to the Spirit and serving God will bring joy and fulfillment on earth, but ultimately it will result in storing up treasures in heaven: "Do not store up for yourselves treasures on earth, where moth and rust destroy, and where thieves break in and steal. But store up for yourselves treasures in heaven, where moth and rust do not destroy, and where thieves do not break in and steal. For where your treasure is, there your heart will be also" (Matt. 6:19–21).

In commenting on this passage, Randy Alcorn said:

> If you stopped reading too soon, you would have thought Christ was against our storing up treasures for ourselves. No. He's all for it! In fact, He *commands* it. Jesus has a treasure mentality. He *wants* us to store up treasures. He's just telling us to stop storing them in the wrong place and start storing them in the right place![8]

223

Amazingly, what we do here on earth directly relates to the treasures we will have in heaven. When we serve others and show kindness to the needy, we earn treasures in heaven. When we use our God-given talents to obey and serve God, we are sending gifts on ahead of us. And we know that God is faithful and will surely keep this promise to us.

Where are you storing up treasures?

Five Pitfalls to Faithful Stewardship

The Scripture passages we have just considered also imply five pitfalls we need to watch out for:

1. Laziness—failing to invest our talents
2. Lack of faithfulness in what we consider small responsibilities
3. Thinking that we ourselves are the source of our gifts and abilities
4. Sowing to the flesh—doing things that serve and please ourselves
5. Striving for earthly treasures—focusing on the present instead of eternity in heaven

As we seek to faithfully steward our talents, let's remember the promises of God to those who are faithful. Let's avoid the pitfalls and lean on the Holy Spirit as we get to work.

A Look in the Mirror

Let's take a few minutes to examine ourselves, to identify our gifts, and to consider how we are investing our talents.

WHAT ARE YOUR GIFTS?

Rate yourself on a scale of 1 to 10. *1 means that you are not gifted at all in this area and 10 means that you have a very strong gifting in this area.*

___ 1. Playing a musical instrument

___ 2. Singing

___ 3. Academics

224

___ 4. Public speaking

___ 5. Teaching

___ 6. Serving and helping others

___ 7. Leadership

___ 8. Leading a small-group discussion

___ 9. Organization and administration

___10. Encouragement

___11. Hospitality—hosting guests or groups

___12. Evangelism

___13. Working with young children

___14. Other: _____

___15. Other: _____

HOW ARE YOU INVESTING YOUR GIFTS?

List your top five gifts from the previous list, and for each one write down ways in which (a) you are currently using your gift and (b) you can use your gift more often.

1. _____

   a. _____

   b. _____

2. _____

   a. _____

   b. _____

3. _____

   a. _____

   b. _____

4. _____

   a. _____

   b. _____

5. _____

    a. _____

    b. _____

Do you have a good understanding of the specific talents that God has given you? Are you currently putting your gifts to work by using them to serve God? Are you looking for more ways to put them into practice to make a greater difference for Christ and his kingdom?

Action Plan

Let's remember that ultimately our focus should be on God—knowing him and growing in our relationship with him—and not ourselves. We need to seek to improve our talents so we can serve him better, and we need to use our gifts because we are motivated by a deep love for our Lord.

Stewardship Tips

We have talked specifically about what stewardship is and why it is important. We have also examined ourselves to evaluate our gifts and how we use them. Let's turn now to practical steps we can take to be more effective stewards of our God-given gifts and abilities.

Here are five tips to Christian stewardship:

1. Enlist the help of others to identify your gifts. We have to know our gifts to fully develop them. We evaluated ourselves earlier in the chapter, but it is important that we also get the opinions of oth-

> **THINK ABOUT IT**
> Before we turn to specific steps we can take to be more effective stewards of our talents, let's consider the following:
>
> God created you with your unique abilities, and He does want to use them. But He's far more interested in you knowing Him than He is you knowing your abilities. The world tells us to affirm self, but God tells us to deny self. Your identity and self-worth aren't found in your abilities, but in your relationship with God.[9] —HENRY AND MEL BLACKABY

ers in this process. We need to ask our parents to look at our self-assessment to see whether they agree and find out whether they have any additional observations. We can do the same with our pastor and any other mature Christians who know us well. The more the circle of individuals we ask expands, the more accurately we will see our gifts. (We should also ask for suggestions on how we can put these gifts to work to serve our family, church, and community.)

All along the way, we need to pray, asking God to clearly show us our talents and ways to invest them. This is a prayer that he is eager to answer.

2. Remember the source. We never want to forget that God is the source of all our abilities, and we never want to get far from him. In John 15:5 Jesus said, "I am the vine; you are the branches. If a man remains in me and I in him, he will bear much fruit; apart from me you can do nothing." Not only is he the original source of our talents, he is also the source of our daily strength as we seek to put them into action.

We need to be people of prayer, thanking God for our gifts and asking him to help us faithfully steward them. We need to look to him for direction so that we can know the best way to put our talents to work, and we need to humbly ask him to increase them all the more.

3. Use them. The best way to steward a gift is to use it. When we lift weights, our muscles get stronger. If we have a gift of leadership, leading will only make us better, especially as we learn from our successes and failures. If we have a musical gift, participating in the choir will stretch us and help us improve. If we have a compassionate heart for the elderly, volunteering to help at a retirement center will teach us how to more effectively care.

The question isn't "Should we put our talents to work?" but rather "How should we put our talents to work?" Faithfully stewarding our gifts means putting them into practice for the glory of God. Our job is to figure out God's assignment for us and then get busy.

227

4. Learn from others. One great aspect of growing up in the church is the many mature Christians from whom we can learn. We need to identify godly individuals who have similar gifts. As we do so, we can carefully observe them and ask them questions. Ask them how they have developed their gifts over the years, and look for ways to spend time with them to learn how they think and act.

5. Seek to be humble. In chapter 5 we discussed the importance of humility. Whenever we consider our gifts and areas of strength in our lives, it is easy to become puffed up. But when we have the mind-set that God is the source of our gifts and he deserves the credit for all that we do, we will remain humble.

Remember 1 Peter 5:5: "God opposes the proud but gives grace to the humble."

With God's help, we can be faithful stewards. We can identify our talents, learn from others, and put them into practice. As we stay rooted and grounded in God, the source of our gifts and strength, we will humbly and effectively bring glory to him. In the end we will hear the Master say, "Well done, good and faithful servant."

A Call to Action

Sometime in the next eighty years—when you die or Christ returns—you will be standing before your Master. He will ask you what you did with the talents he entrusted to you. What will you say to him? God calls you to be a faithful steward of the gifts and abilities he has given you. As a church kid, you have been given much, and much is required of you. Are you ready to get to work?

Commit today to:

√ Glorify God by faithfully managing your talents

√ Look for ways to use and develop your gifts and abilities

√ Remember that God is the source of all your talents and will provide the strength you need to put them to work in his kingdom

Questions for Reflection and Discussion

1. What does it mean to steward your gifts, talents, and abilities?

2. What aspects of stewardship did the financial investment chart highlight?

3. What challenges do church kids face in stewarding their talents?

4. What is the main point of the parable of the talents?

5. What is the connection between being faithful in little and being faithful in much? What are some little things in your life in which you need to be faithful right now?

6. What are the two sides of the sowing-and-reaping principle outlined in Galatians 6:7–9? What are examples of sowing to the sinful nature? Sowing to the Spirit?

7. What does it mean to store up treasures in heaven? What is one thing you can do that will store up treasures in heaven?

8. Which stewardship pitfall seems to trip you up the most?

9. What is one talent that God has given you? How can you put it to work in your home, church, or community?

10. How can your parents and pastor help you identify and develop your talents?

11. What does John 15:5 mean? Why is this important to keep in mind as you walk out the Christian life?

12. Who is one mature Christian with a talent similar to one of yours? What could you ask him or her that would help you to develop and use your talent?

Sing a New Song

"As Long as I Have Breath"[10]

How do I thank You, oh Lord
For taking my place on the cross
And how do I thank You, oh Lord
For all of Your mercy and kindness
For calling me to You
For letting me hear You
For opening my heart to the Gospel

Chorus
As long as I have breath I will praise You
As long as my heart beats I will sing
As long as life flows in my veins
I will bless Your name

How do I thank You, oh Lord
For all of the love in Your eyes
And how do I thank You, oh Lord
For how You have changed me forever
For giving me power
And hope and a future
With favor and gladness and every good
thing

For more information on this song, go to www.growingupchristian.com.

230

NOTES

Chapter 1: Church Kids

1. J. C. Ryle, *Holiness* (Moscow, Idaho: Charles Nolan, 2001), 199.
2. Steve Earl, "Haven't You Been Good," Sovereign Grace Worship (ASCAP), 1998.

Chapter 2: In or Out?

1. http://www.cnn.com/2002/LAW/05/10/spy.hanssen/index.html.
2. http://www.cnn.com/2001/US/02/21/spy.profile/index.html.
3. Ibid.
4. http://www.cnn.com/2002/LAW/05/10/spy.hanssen/index.html.
5. Paraphrase of John Owen, *Communion with God* (Carlisle, Pa.: Banner of Truth, 1991), 36.
6. Catherine Marshall, *Christy* (New York: Avon Books, 1968), 331.
7. Charles Spurgeon, *Morning and Evening* (Fearn, Ross-shire, Scotland: Christian Focus), Evening, December, 2000.
8. Ibid., Evening, December 30, 2000.
9. Randy Alcorn, *The Grace and Truth Paradox* (Sisters, Ore.: Multnomah, 2003), 38.
10. As described in the hymn "Tell Me the Old, Old Story" by Katherine Hankey.
11. Paraphrase of Spurgeon, *Morning and Evening*, Evening, December 18, 2000.
12. Lyrics by Charitie Lees Bancroft, "Before the Throne of God Above." Music and alternate lyrics by Vikki Cook, Sovereign Grace Worship (ASCAP), 1997.

Chapter 3: Un-Amazing Grace

1. Jerry Bridges, *Transforming Grace* (Colorado Springs: NavPress, 1991), 21–22.
2. Randy Alcorn, *The Grace and Truth Paradox* (Sisters, Ore.: Multnomah, 2003), 31–32.

3. Ibid., 33.

4. Wayne Grudem, *Systematic Theology* (Grand Rapids: Zondervan, 1994), chs. 11–13.

5. J. C. Ryle, *Holiness* (Moscow, Idaho: Charles Nolan, 2001).

6. J. I. Packer, *Knowing God* (Downers Grove, Ill.: InterVarsity Press, 1973).

7. Randy Alcorn, *The Grace and Truth Paradox* (Sisters, Ore.: Multnomah, 2003), 44–45.

8. John Owen, *The Works of John Owen*, vol. 6 (Carlisle, Pa.: Banner of Truth, 1995).

9. Chris Lundgaard, *The Enemy Within* (Phillipsburg, N.J.: P&R, 1998).

10. The lyrics for a great song are given at the end of this chapter.

11. Steve and Vikki Cook, "I Will Glory in My Redeemer," Sovereign Grace Worship (ASCAP), 2000.

Chapter 4: The Cost of Compromise

1. John Piper, *A Hunger for God* (Wheaton, Ill.: Crossway, 1997), 14.

2. C. S. Lewis, *The Screwtape Letters* (New York: HarperCollins, 2001), 61.

3. Jerry Bridges, *The Discipline of Grace* (Colorado Springs: NavPress, 1994), 202–3.

4. J. C. Ryle, *Holiness* (Moscow, Idaho: Charles Nolan, 2001), 64.

5. Bridges, *Discipline of Grace*, 209.

6. We will further examine battling sin in chapter 10.

7. Piper, *A Hunger for God*, 23.

8. Steve and Vikki Cook, "You Have Captured Me," Sovereign Grace Worship (ASCAP), 2000.

Chapter 5: Biblical Greatness

1. *Remember the Titans*, Walt Disney Pictures, stock no. 22853.

2. Jerry Bridges, *The Practice of Godliness* (Colorado Springs: NavPress, 1996), 73–74.

3. Ibid., 81.

4. Wayne Grudem, *Systematic Theology* (Grand Rapids: Zondervan, 1994), 162.

5. http://www.forbes.com/static/bill2005/rank.html.

6. I acknowledge my debt to my friend Kevin Hartnett, who works for the Hubble Telescope Program at NASA.

7. Steve and Vikki Cook, "I Bow Down," Sovereign Grace Worship (ASCAP), 1999.

Chapter 6: More Than Mimicking Mom and Dad

1. In Touch Ministries, "Eric Liddell: Running the Race," www.intouch.org/myintouch/mighty/portraits/eric_liddell_213688.html.

2. Christian History Institute, "Eric Liddell: Champion Athlete Devoted to God; His Life Was Much More than a Race for Olympic Gold," issue no. 161, www.gospelcom.net/chi/GLIMPSEF/Glimpses/glmps161.shtml.

3. Josh McDowell and Bob Hostetler, *Beyond Belief to Convictions* (Wheaton, Ill.: Tyndale, 2002), 7.

4. Ibid., 6–7.

5. George Barna, *Real Teens* (Ventura, Calif.: Regal, 2001), 131–32. The national studies took place in 1999 and 2000.

6. Jerry Bridges, *The Discipline of Grace* (Colorado Springs: NavPress, 1994), 162.

7. McDowell and Hostetler, *Beyond Belief*, 22.

8. Catherine Marshall, *Christy* (New York: Avon Books, 1968), 296–97.

9. Ibid., 434.

10. Mark Altrogge, "For Your Glory Alone," Sovereign Grace Praise, 1999.

Chapter 7: Familiar Yet Thankful

1. "Experimental Surgery Zaps Tourette's Tics" http://abcnews.go.com/GMA /DrJohnson/story?id=127925&page=1.

2. Ibid.

3. D. A. Carson, *Matthew*, The Expositor's Bible Commentary 8 (Grand Rapids: Zondervan, 1984), 328.

4. Joni Eareckson Tada, *Joni* (Grand Rapids: Zondervan, 2001), 13–15.

5. Ibid., 187–88.

6. Jerry Bridges, *The Practice of Godliness* (Colorado Springs: NavPress, 1996), 105.

7. In chapter 11 we will discuss our need to practice the spiritual disciplines for the purpose of growing in our relationship with God.

8. Bridges, *Practice of Godliness*, 100.

9. Randy Alcorn, *The Grace and Truth Paradox* (Sisters, Ore.: Multnomah, 2003), 84.

10. Mark Altrogge, "I Stand in Awe," Sovereign Grace Praise, 1986.

Chapter 8: Building a Firm Foundation

1. Randy Alcorn, *The Grace and Truth Paradox* (Sisters, Ore.: Multnomah, 2003), 37.

2. J. C. Ryle, *Holiness* (Moscow, Idaho: Charles Nolan, 2001), 86–87.

3. Ibid., 90.

4. I acknowledge my debt to Ken Burns's documentary *The Brooklyn Bridge*, 1981.

5. Alcorn, *Grace and Truth Paradox*, 58.

6. J. I. Packer, *Knowing God* (Downers Grove, Ill.: InterVarsity Press, 1993), 21.

7. Ibid., 23.

8. Wayne Grudem, *Bible Doctrine* (Grand Rapids: Zondervan, 1999).

9. Lyrics by Isaac Watts, "Join All the Glorious Names." Music and alternate lyrics by Bob Kauflin, Sovereign Grace Praise (BMI), 2000.

Chapter 9: Banking on God

1. Jerry Bridges, *Trusting God* (Colorado Springs: NavPress, 1988), 201–2.

2. J. I. Packer, *Knowing God* (Downers Grove, Ill.: InterVarsity Press, 1973), 83.

3. Ibid., 91.

4. John Stott, *The Cross of Christ* (Downers Grove, Ill.: InterVarsity Press, 1986), 328–29.

5. Packer, *Knowing God*, 97.

6. Bridges, *Trusting God*.

7. Packer, *Knowing God*.

8. Wayne Grudem, *Bible Doctrine* (Grand Rapids: Zondervan, 1999).

9. Steve and Vikki Cook, "O Wondrous Love," Sovereign Grace Worship (ASCAP), 2001.

Chapter 10: The Fight of Your Life

1. *The Washington Post*, May 2, 2003.

2. J. C. Ryle, *Holiness* (Moscow, Idaho: Charles Nolan, 2001), 63.

3. Elyse Fitzpatrick, *Idols of the Heart* (Phillipsburg, N.J.: P&R, 2001), 101.

4. John Owen, *Temptation and Sin* (Carlisle, Pa.: Banner of Truth, 1995), 7.

5. Wayne Grudem, *Systematic Theology* (Grand Rapids: Zondervan, 1994), 490.

6. Ryle, *Holiness*, 2.

7. Kris Lundgaard, *The Enemy Within* (Phillipsburg, N.J.: P&R, 1998), 33.

8. Owen, *Temptation and Sin*, 12.

9. Lundgaard, *The Enemy Within*, 45–46.

10. Owen, *Temptation and Sin*, 7.

11. Jerry Bridges, *The Pursuit of Holiness* (Colorado Springs: NavPress, 1996), 84–85.

12. Words by Augustus Toplady, "Rock of Ages." Music and alternate lyrics by Bob Kauflin, Sovereign Grace Praise (BMI), 1998.

Chapter 11: Spiritual Push-ups

1. Adapted from Luke 19:1–10.

2. The opening story was inspired by Donald Whitney, *Spiritual Disciplines for the Christian Life* (Colorado Springs: NavPress, 1991), 19.

3. Ibid., 18.

4. Ibid., 20.

5. Ibid., 21.

6. Jerry Bridges, *The Practice of Godliness* (Colorado Springs: NavPress, 1996), 51.

7. J. C. Ryle, *Holiness* (Moscow, Idaho: Charles Nolan, 2001), 110.

8. Jerry Bridges, *The Discipline of Grace* (Colorado Springs: NavPress, 1994), 134.

9. Whitney, *Spiritual Disciplines for the Christian Life*, 28.

10. Words by Eric Grover, music by Eric Grover, "Your Great Renown," Sovereign Grace Praise (BMI), and Steve Cook, Sovereign Grace Worship (ASCAP), 1998.

Chapter 12: Making the Most of It

1. Louis Auchincloss, *Theodore Roosevelt* (New York: Times Books, Henry Holt and Company, 2001), 12.

2. "Theodore Roosevelt." Online: www.ushistory.net/toc/roosevelt.html.

3. Tweed Roosevelt, "Theodore Roosevelt: A Brief Biography," www.theodore roosevelt.org/life/biotr.htm.

4. Ibid.

5. Randy Alcorn, *The Treasure Principle* (Sisters, Ore.: Multnomah, 2001), 24.

6. J. C. Ryle, *Holiness* (Moscow, Idaho: Charles Nolan, 2001), 173.

7. Henry and Mel Blackaby, *What's So Spiritual about Your Gifts?* (Sisters, Ore.: Multnomah, 2004), 23.

8. Alcorn, *The Treasure Principle*, 15.

9. Blackaby, *What's So Spiritual about Your Gifts?*, 29.

10. Mark Altrogge, "As Long as I Have Breath,"Sovereign Grace Praise, 1998.

Karl Graustein is the high school principal at Covenant Life School in Gaithersburg, Maryland, where he has been serving for the past eight years. Before moving to Maryland, Karl taught for four years at Laconia Christian School in Laconia, New Hampshire—the school he attended K-12. Karl earned a bachelor's degree from Wheaton College in 1993 and a master's degree from Regent University in 1997. He and his wife, Jennifer, and their two girls, Anna and Sarah, live in Gaithersburg, Maryland, and attend Covenant Life Church (www.covlife.org).

My church belongs to a group of churches called Sovereign Grace Ministries, which aims to start, establish, and strengthen local churches. You can visit their website at **www.SovereignGraceMinistries.org**. Be sure to check out their great worship music. Here are a few of my favorites.

Worship God Live

Our latest release, *Worship God Live,* features 14 new songs celebrating the grace and majesty of God. Recorded with hundreds of worshipers during two evenings at Covenant Life Church, it is our first live CD in six years. "We recorded some wonderful, Christ-exalting, God-centered songs, and were able to capture some of the enthusiasm and spontaneity of a live context," says Bob Kauflin, one of two worship leaders on the CD.

All We Long To See

A life lived for Another—for the One who died, and rose, and will come again—is a life marked by eager anticipation, holy yearning, joyful praise. *All We Long to See* explores the worship experience of the Christian who has been captivated by God's grace and mercy displayed at the cross. Come be reminded of what matters most. Come be encouraged and exhorted. Come and worship Him who is worthy of all praise.

Songs for the Cross Centered Life

This worship CD was inspired by a little, orange book called *The Cross Centered Life*, by C.J. Mahaney (soon to be issued in an expanded version called *Living the Cross Centered Life*). The CD booklet contains the entire first chapter, making the project an inspiring reminder of how to preach the gospel to ourselves.What the book does in print, this CD does in 14 cross-centered songs, five of which are new and nine are updated favorites from earlier recordings.

Upward: The Bob Kauflin Hymns Project

Have you realized that hymns don't have to be boring? That they really can speak with power? Bob selected, adapted, and arranged these songs— some of them familiar, some new, and some newly revised. Each one directs our gaze upward to our magnificent God and Savior. Featuring diverse musical styles, plus a devotional from Bob for each song, here is life-changing truth—exactly what hymns were meant to be.

I Stand in Awe: Favorites From PDI Music

This worship compilation from Sovereign Grace Music (released under our former music label, PDI Music) presents 12 of the best songs, newly rearranged and re-recorded, from the nearly 300 praise & worship songs published by Sovereign Grace since the mid-1980s.

SOVEREIGN GRACE®
MINISTRIES